discover art

AT DUBLIN CITY GALLERY THE HUGH LANE

AN INTRODUCTION TO MODERN AND CONTEMPORARY ART FOR YOUNG PEOPLE

Jessica O'Donnell

For Nora, Jesse, Finn, Louis and Lucy.

First published 2007
Second edition 2008 by
Dublin City Gallery The Hugh Lane
Charlemont House
Parnell Square North
Dublin 1

Cover image: Big Bird by Niki de Saint Phalle,
© ADAGP, Paris and DACS, London 2007
Photographs of artworks by John Kellett except pps.16,17, 20,
39, 54, 60, 61, 62 National Gallery, London.
Photograph of Enda Wyley, p. 64 by Iarla O Lionáird.
Photographs of gallery exterior and entrance pps. 11 and 45
by Barry Mason Photography.
Photographs pps. 8-9, 27, 28, 47, 53, 59, 72, 95, 98-99, and
back cover by Jessica O'Donnell.

Illustration p. 22 by Felicity Clear
Art Activity illustrations by contributing artists pps. 23-24,
30-31, 37, 63, 73, 78.
Drawings p.13 by D. Skelly and S. Linehan.
Cartoon character and cartoon drawings by Fever Interactive
with additional drawings by IRN Publishing Ltd.

Municipal Gallery Favourite (After Patrick Scott) by Enda
Wyley was published in *Eating Baby Jesus*, Dedalus Press,
Dublin 1994.

Proof reader: Elizabeth Mayes.

ISBN 1901702 26 X (PB)
ISBN 1901702 286 (HB)

Produced by MB Solutions
Designed by IRN Publishing LTD
Colour reproduction and printing by Nicholson & Bass

100 YEARS

Department of Arts, Sport and Tourism
An Roinn Ealaíon, Spóirt agus Turasóireachta

HUGH LANE

Dublin City Council
Comhairle Cathrach Bhaile Átha Cliath

Contents

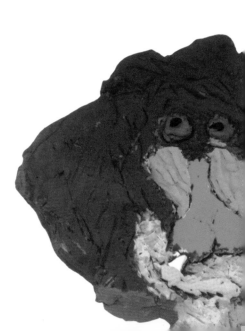

Lord Mayor's Preface

Dublin City Gallery The Hugh Lane was founded in 1908 due to the vision and perseverance of Hugh Lane and his friends, and to their deeply held belief that Irish and international modern art deserved to be seen, celebrated and appreciated by all the people of Dublin. While arts education is a relatively new discipline in Ireland, their pervading, essentially educational, philosophy has guided the gallery ever since its foundation.

With direction, the arts can play a crucial role in encouraging young people to fulfil their potential, enhance their self-esteem, their self-awareness, their social and linguistic skills. Art workshops encourage young people's creativity and self-expression; they are a time to have fun together!

Above all, looking at art can unlock young people's imagination and critical thinking. It can be daunting to be confronted with an artwork without knowing how to approach it or what to make of it. It is here that the role of the gallery's education programme, which promotes understanding, participation and appreciation is such an essential function of the gallery.

Dublin City Council's commitment to youth affairs and young people is demonstrated by the publication of our *Youth Affairs Strategy and Action Plan 2006-2009*. Testament to the gallery's commitment to arts education in the city is the wonderful dedicated children's area and education resource room located in the Hugh Lane's new extension. It is our intention to further realise the potential of this space, to increase access and participation by young people and to respond to the exciting changes that are rapidly taking place within our city. This publication will make a valuable contribution to raising awareness of the treasures of Dublin City Gallery The Hugh Lane and to achieving these important goals.

Vincent Jackson

The Lord Mayor of Dublin, **Cllr. Vincent Jackson**

Director's Foreword

Introducing new audiences to the visual arts is both a delight and a challenge. This book is a stimulating introduction to modern and contemporary art. Drawing on the gallery's prodigious collection, including Francis Bacon's studio, we are presented, in a lively and informative text, with the concerns that preoccupied artists from the turn of the 20th century until today.

From the history of the founding of the gallery by Hugh Lane to starting your own collection, the reader is encouraged to look at the artworks from their own perspective, becoming an art detective! Artists at work, drawing, art and music, art and poetry are all explored in an innovative way through image and language. Beautifully illustrated, the questions posed and activities included in each chapter encourage individual participation. It is a must for any young person who enjoys art.

Figurative and abstract painting is discussed and explained, as well as sculpture and new media, including film and photography. These new art forms are central to contemporary art practice and are of additional inspiration to budding young artists.

Discover Art brings us on a unique journey through the process and realisation of visual arts practice by the great artists of the past and of today. It is a celebration of the role that art plays in our development and education, drawing out the unique expression that is in each of us.

Congratulations to Jessica O'Donnell, author of *Discover Art* at Dublin City Gallery The Hugh Lane, for writing such a thoughtful, exciting book for young people. Her dedication to a contemporary approach to art and education is very evident in her illuminating text.

Barbara Dawson
Director

About this Book

Dublin City Gallery The Hugh Lane has a wonderful collection of Irish and international modern and contemporary art. *Discover Art* offers an enjoyable and lively introduction for young people to the collection of this gallery. In addition parents and teachers may also find this book to be a helpful resource. Each chapter includes ideas for practical art activities, contributed by artists who have worked closely with the gallery's education programme. This programme sees emerging artists, in discussion with the gallery's Education Curator, devise and implement innovative workshops for families and schools, inspired by the permanent collection and temporary exhibitions and informed by the artists' own practice. The art activities described and illustrated here are drawn from these popular programmes, or are a variation on similar workshop themes. As such, they have been tried and tested by children themselves, as well as by teachers during our in-service workshop programmes.

The thematic approach of this book is intended to bring the reader through the gallery by suggesting comparisons of artists and artistic styles from different periods within the collection. This approach has grown out of the responses and experiences of our many visiting groups, from activity sheets and painting guides for children developed in-house, as well as from articles on the collection written for *Classmate,* Dublin City Council's magazine for primary schools. In addition to paintings, sculpture, film and works on paper, insights into the art-making process are also explored. In this way, it is hoped, many avenues into art are presented for the younger visitor.

Each of the artworks discussed is illustrated and art terms are explained where they arise within the relevant chapters. There is also a glossary and an index of artists accompanied by relevant page numbers for easy reference to particular artists. Practical information on visiting the gallery is included and the book is ideal both for preparation in advance of a proposed visit or as a follow up at home or in the classroom.

To encourage looking at and responding to artworks, questions are suggested as spurs to offering an opinion in the *Be an Art Detective* pages. The **i** and **?** symbols together with the **Art**trivia boxes are further little pointers to stimulate discussion.

Enjoy this book and your visits to Dublin City Gallery The Hugh Lane!

Acknowledgements

It is always a pleasure to work with gifted emerging artists and I wish to thank the following artists who have contributed such lovely ideas for art activities to this book:

Felicity Clear *Making mini Francis Bacon studios; Making your own artist's sketchbook; Making an ornate frame; Making large-scale portraits.*

Kitty Rogers *A textured landscape; Autumn falling leaves; Making a fairytale stained glass banner; Winter bonnets.*

Beth O'Halloran *Cherry blossoms; Tonal stories.*

Wendy Judge *Make a pop-up spiral*

Gillian Field *Painting multi-coloured butterflies*

Máire Davey *How to make a pin-hole camera*

I would like to thank Barbara Dawson, Director, for providing me with the opportunity to write this book and for her ongoing support of the project; the support received from Katy Fitzpatrick, Liz Forster, Joanna Shepard and my colleagues at the gallery is much appreciated; my sincere thanks to Enda Wyley for her wonderful contribution to the *Art and Poetry* chapter recollecting her childhood visits to the Hugh Lane, her suggestions for poetry and art activities and for permission to reproduce her poem *Municipal Gallery Favourite (After Patrick Scott)*; to all the artists and artists' estates for their generosity and kindness in giving permission to reproduce their work, I am very thankful; my thanks also to Kim Willoughby with whom it has been very enjoyable to work on the design of this book; to Anne Ryan, St. Paul's JNS; to Shane Hallahan, Manager of the gallery bookshop for his helpful advice; and to my parents for their support and encouragement.

A special word of thanks is due to all the artists, guides and workshop assistants who have participated in Hugh Lane education programmes. With the valuable and much appreciated support of the gallery attendants, their talent, enthusiasm and commitment have ensured the success of our children's workshop programme to date.

Jessica O'Donnell

About the Gallery

Dublin City Gallery The Hugh Lane is a gallery of modern and contemporary art. The gallery has a wonderful collection of painting and sculpture dating from the mid-19th century to today. Have you ever seen a couch made with thousands of hairclips, oil paint squeezed onto a canvas in thick colourful blobs or one of the smallest horses in the world? Well, you can at Dublin City Gallery The Hugh Lane.

Portrait of Hugh Lane
by John Singer Sargent

The gallery is named after Hugh Lane, an art dealer and collector, who was born in Cork in 1875. Hugh Lane's aunt was Lady Augusta Gregory (1852-1932), a leading figure in the Irish Celtic Revival. Hugh Lane loved art and he bought and sold paintings in London. He believed that there should be a gallery of modern art in Dublin representing the best of Irish and international artists. Together with his friends, Lane established the Municipal Gallery of Modern Art in 1908 in Harcourt Street in Dublin.

In 1915 Hugh Lane died at the young age of 39 when the *Lusitania*, the ship on which he was travelling on his way back from a visit to America, was torpedoed by a German U-boat off the coast of Cork and sunk.

In 1933 the Municipal Art Gallery, as it was then known, moved to Charlemont House in Parnell Square where it is today. Originally Lord Charlemont's townhouse, Charlemont House was designed by the architect Sir William Chambers (1723-1796) and was built in 1765. Look out for the wonderful plasterwork and elegant fireplaces during your visit.

The exterior of Dublin City Gallery The Hugh Lane

Recently, a large extension was built to the gallery resulting in more space for the permanent collection and temporary exhibitions, a lovely children's area and education resource space for fun art workshops, a larger bookshop and a lively café.

One of the gallery's interior staircases

The entrance hall of the gallery

Visiting the Gallery

Dublin City Gallery The Hugh Lane is located on Parnell Square North, which is at the top of Dublin's main street, O'Connell Street. The Dart, Luas and a large number of buses all pass close to the gallery. The gallery is completely wheelchair accessible and there are lifts to all floors. Should you wish to visit the gallery with your class, guided tours and special artist-led workshops may be booked by

Sean Scully Room

contacting the gallery's Education Department at least two weeks in advance of your proposed visit. You can also make a virtual visit through the gallery's website **www.hughlane.ie**. Here you will find illustrations of artworks in the collection as well as details of exhibitions, family art workshops, lectures and special events.

While reproductions and posters are a very good way of studying or admiring your favourite works of art at home or in the classroom, there is no comparison with visiting a gallery and looking at real paintings and sculptures. Sometimes artworks are surprisingly larger or smaller than you expected or colours and brushstrokes are more textured and vibrant. When looking at paintings in the gallery you can study them up close or from a distance. With sculpture you can walk around it and look at it from different angles.

Looking at artworks in this way can change the way they appear and also lead to new discoveries!

REMEMBER!
It is always important not to touch any of the artworks in the gallery. Paintings and sculpture are unique objects which are delicate and fragile.

Drawing after *Beach Scene South of France* by William J. Leech and drawing after
Southern Window by Louis le Brocquy both made during Sunday Sketching workshops.

Art Workshops for Children

One of the most enjoyable ways of exploring the collection of the gallery is to
participate in one of the many family and schools art workshops that take place
regularly.

Be an Art Detective
Some questions to ask!

* Is it a painting, a sculpture, a drawing, a print, an installation, a film or a photograph?

* How old is the work? When was it made?

* Who made it?

* What is it made of?

* Why was it made?

* Who was it made for?

* Is the work signed? Where is it signed?

* What is taking place? Is a story being told?

* Is it a portrait, a landscape, a seascape, a townscape, abstract, a still life?

* Does the work look realistic?
  Does the artist want it to look realistic? Has the artist exaggerated the way something looks or the colours and brushstrokes they are using?

* Is the work painted in an expressive manner? Look at the brushstrokes, colours, lighting and subject.

* Describe the colour, tone and texture you see.

* What is the light like in the painting? Is there a strong contrast between light and shade? What shapes and patterns do you see?

* Is it a large or small work? What effect does the scale have on the work and have on you?

* How would you describe the mood of the work? How does the choice of colours affect the mood of the work?

* Do you like it? Why? Why not?

* How does the artwork compare with others in the same room? Are there any connections between the artworks?

* Would you have chosen to show this work? Why? Why not?

* Would you have displayed this artwork in a different way? How?

* Has the artist used a lot of different colours or chosen to use only a few or even only one?

* Describe the gestures, expressions and clothes in the work. How do these help to tell a story?

* Do you think the work was made in the artist's studio or out of doors?

* If it is a painting of a person or people, are there objects in the painting which help to tell us more about them – for example who they are, their interests, their job?

* If you could own one artwork in the gallery, which would it be?

* Was the work made to record a special event or place, to express a new idea, to experiment with different styles, subjects and techniques, to make a political or artistic statement?

* Are the lines and shapes in the work angular, curved, straight, crooked, blurred?

* Does the work look different when looked at up close and from a distance?

* Can you walk around the work and look at it from different angles or does the artist want you to view it from a particular point such as from below, from the side, from above or from the front?

* Do you think the work was made quickly?

* Do you think it would have taken the artist a long time to make the work?

* Do you think it was difficult to make the work?

* Would the artist have needed help or technical assistance from other people?

* Is the artist using traditional artists' materials or unusual materials such as found items or everyday objects?

* Are there ways that the work interacts with the viewer – for example, in a painting are there people looking out directly at you, in an installation or sculpture are there mechanical devices that make a sound or move when someone comes near or are the surfaces reflective so that you can see yourself in them?

* Has the artist made other versions of the subject? How do they compare with the artwork?

Art Activity

I SPY WITH MY LITTLE EYE
Test your art observational skills by playing I Spy!
Choose a painting or room in the gallery and with a friend take turns to lead.

I spy with my little eye something beginning with .....

Art Collections

The permanent collection of a gallery grows over time through the acquisition of artworks by purchases, donations and bequests. Donations or bequests are when people give an artwork as a gift to a gallery. Occasionally a person may loan an artwork for a fixed period of time for the public to enjoy, after which time the artwork is returned to its owner.

The Umbrellas
(Les Parapluies)
by Auguste Renoir

At the time the original collection of this gallery was being established, Hugh Lane wrote to many artists asking them to donate examples of their work. Many did just this or offered their work at very low prices. During his lifetime, Hugh Lane bought many of the most renowned paintings in the gallery. Not least among these are paintings by 19th century continental artists including *Les Parapluies* by Auguste Renoir, *Music in the Tuileries Gardens* by Edouard Manet and *Beach Scene (Bains de mer: petite fille peignée par sa bonne)* by Edgar Degas which form part of the Hugh Lane Bequest. These paintings are now among the most famous paintings in the world.

The Mantlepiece (La Cheminée)
by Edouard Vuillard

Because of the controversy and delay about finding a suitable building and location of a gallery to house his collection, Hugh Lane grew impatient and decided to give thirty-nine of what he considered to be among his best paintings to the National Gallery, London.

Following Hugh Lane's premature death in 1915, there was confusion surrounding an un-witnessed codicil which he had made to his will. A **codicil** is a change or

Beach Scene
(Bains de mer: petite fille peignée par sa bonne)
by Edgar Degas

addition to a will. An agreement has since been reached where these thirty-nine paintings originally owned by Hugh Lane are exhibited in turn by the National Gallery, London and Dublin City Gallery The Hugh Lane.

Art Activity

START YOUR OWN COLLECTION

Why not start your own collection of objects? Begin by choosing a category of objects that interests you. For example, stickers, rubbers, pebbles, shells, stamps, buttons, coloured glass, leaves, dried flowers, old perfume bottles, comics or badges.

Then collect examples of your chosen category which have different colours, designs, ages, rarity or uniqueness. You could swap examples with other young collectors of similar objects.

As the variety of your collection grows some interesting examples may provide inspiration for your drawings or paintings. You could also use your collection as the basis for a mini-exhibition for your family or in the classroom.

Write little explanatory labels to accompany the objects in your mini-exhibition.

> LOUIS LE BROCQUY
> b. Dublin 1916
>
> HEAD AND HORIZON 1960
>
> Oil on canvas 114.3 x 146 cm
>
> Presented by the Contemporary Irish Art Society, 1966
>
> Reg. 1257

This is an example of a painting label used in the gallery.

The Artist at Work

Interior of Francis Bacon Studio, 7 Reece Mews
by Perry Ogden

Francis Bacon often
used plates as
palettes

An artist's studio is the name of the room where an artist paints, sculpts, draws or just sits and thinks of ideas!

The Francis Bacon Studio

Francis Bacon was one of the most famous artists of the 20th century. Although he lived most of his life in London, he was born in Dublin and lived in Co. Kildare with his family until he was 16 years of age. He liked being surrounded by lots of things as he could then easily reach for one of his many art books, photographs or newspaper clippings in search of inspiration. His studio contained over 7,500

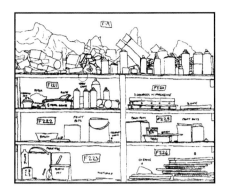

This archaeologist's drawing was used to record the location of items found in Francis Bacon's studio and to assist with the re-construction of the studio in Dublin.

items including paint pots, brushes, two easels and a mirror. He used the walls and door of his studio as a palette and these are covered in blobs of pink, red, orange among other colour paint. Very few people were allowed into the room especially when he was working. Following Francis Bacon's death, his studio was donated to the gallery by his friend John Edwards. Like a large-scale jigsaw, the entire studio was then moved from London to Dublin and put back together exactly the way it was. By studying the items found in his studio, discoveries have been made about what and how he painted.

One of the palette knives found in Francis Bacon's Studio

Portrait of Miss Anstruther Thomson
by John Singer Sargent

John Singer Sargent was one of the most famous portrait painters of his day. He was very skilled at painting the magnificent dresses that were fashionable during the late 19th century and early 20th century. In this black chalk drawing, he shows Miss Anstruther Thomson holding a pencil in her hand and a sketchbook on her lap. She is wearing a long dress with very full, puffy sleeves. There is a lot of light coming in from a side window. She is concentrating very hard on what she is drawing. What do you think she may be sketching?

Miss Anstruther Thomson by John Singer Sargent

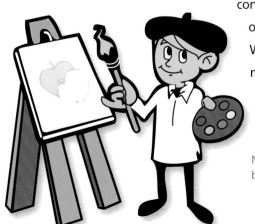

Portrait of Eva Gonzalès by Edouard Manet

Eva Gonzalès was a young French artist who was a dear friend and pupil of Edouard Manet. In this very large work, Eva is shown painting a vase of flowers in her studio. One of the flowers, a white peony, has fallen to the floor. Around her are all the things Eva needs to paint: an easel to hold her painting, a palette to mix and test her colours and a selection of paintbrushes of different sizes. Having brushes of different sizes meant that she could use some for little details and the larger ones for the background. She is also holding a long stick. This is called a *mahl* stick. She used this to lean on and keep her hand steady while she carefully painted the little petals. Leaning against her chair is a portfolio containing some of her paintings and drawings. Eva is wearing a beautiful white dress. She probably wanted to wear her best outfit because she was having her portrait painted. However, white may not be the best colour to wear while she is painting!

Portrait of Eva Gonzalès
by Edouard Manet

Still Life is the name given to paintings of flowers, fruit or objects.

The Artist's Studio by James McNeill Whistler

This is one of two sketches Whistler made showing himself at work in his studio which he intended to use as studies for a large oil painting. This oil sketch shows Whistler standing with a palette in his hand. His palette had raised edges to stop runny paint from dripping onto the floor. There are two elegant women in his studio. Whistler loved all things Japanese and in this painting one of the women is holding a fan and wearing a kimono. The woman sitting down was an Irish woman called Joanna Heffernan. She was the artist's model.

The Artist's Studio
by James McNeill Whistler

Unusual Working Methods: Antonio Mancini

Hugh Lane had his portrait painted by the Italian artist Antonio Mancini during a visit to Rome in 1904. Impressed with the result, Lane invited Mancini to Dublin. A special studio was set up for Mancini in a large room in Clonmell House in Harcourt Street, the first home of the Municipal Gallery of Modern Art. When painting portraits, Mancini had a very distinctive way of working to help him get a good likeness. First of all he would set up a frame in front of the person he was painting. He would then pin criss-cross threads to the frame to create a grid made up of lots of squares. He would place another similar shaped grid very close to his own canvas. Then square-by-square he painted through this thread grid. The grid helped him compose his painting and ensure that everything was the right size and in proportion. Because he used such thick oil paint, many of his paintings have this grid shape imprinted on the painted surface. He was careful, however, to avoid these square shapes appearing on the faces of the people he was painting.

Composing a Picture: Composition is a word to describe how a picture is arranged, where objects or people are placed and what is chosen to be included.

 **Art**trivia

Berthe Morisot used to paint in her drawing room and would tidy her equipment away in a cupboard when visitors called.

Portrait of Lady Gregory by Antonio Mancini

The portrait shows Mancini's distinctive grid square shapes

ARTISTS' EQUIPMENT

Paintings: Out of necessity, artists occasionally used materials which were easily and cheaply available. The French artist Paul Gauguin, for example, is known to have painted on potato sacks stretched over a wooden frame. However, most of the paintings in the gallery are painted on canvas. Canvas is usually made of linen which has been stretched over a wooden frame. Occasionally canvas can also be made of hemp, jute or cotton. A *primer* or *ground* spread over the canvas protects the paint surface and gives it a smooth finish. It also prevents paint from sinking into the fabric. The colour of the *primer* or *ground* can influence the tonal range or overall colour of the painting. In addition to paintings on canvas, there are paintings on cardboard, wood, aluminium, zinc, copper, porcelain and a synthetic wood material called MDF in the gallery's collection. Oil paint, acrylic paint, household paint, watercolour, gold leaf, sand, gouache and gesso are among the materials artists have used. Sometimes artists varnish their paintings to give them a protective layer and a finished appearance. Over time, varnish can sometimes discolour and make colours seem darker than they are.

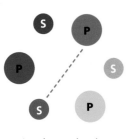

A colour wheel: Primary and Secondary colours

Brushes: These are a selection of brushes used by artists. Brushes are not the only implements used by artists to apply paint. Oil paint can also be added to the canvas with a palette knife or squeezed directly from a tube. Jack B. Yeats often used a palette knife for his oil paintings. Large roller and household brushes, as well as aerosol spray cans, were among the unusual methods of applying paint employed by Francis Bacon.

Jam jar: to hold any liquids to dilute your paint or clean your paintbrushes

Palette: Useful to mix and test your colours. Yellow, Red and Blue are called **primary** colours because they cannot be made from any other colours. Orange, green and purple are called **secondary** colours because they can be made by mixing two primary colours together.

> **i**
>
> Francis Bacon preferred to paint on an unprimed canvas because it had a rougher texture.

i

Complementary colours are those which are opposite each other on the colour wheel.

Art Activity

MAKING MINI FRANCIS BACON STUDIOS

First visit the Francis Bacon studio. Walk all around it. Look through the door, the spy holes and the window. In a notebook or on a piece of paper write or sketch the following information which will help you make your mini-studio:

1. What is covering the floor?
2. What coloured paint is on the walls?
3. What shape are the windows?
4. List five objects you can see in the studio e.g. books, easel, mirror and so on.

What you need:

* Shoe box with lid
* Poster paints or crayons
* Magazines and/or newspapers
* Tin foil for the mirror
* Sheets of acetate or plastic for windows (optional)
* Card
* Scissors
* Glue

Instructions:

* The shoe box represents the studio. First you need to cut out the window at one of the short ends of the shoe box. Some adult help may be needed here. You can also cut out a door along one of the sides and another larger window in the lid of the box.

* Next you can fill the interior of the box based on the information you collected during your visit. Start by covering the floor with bits of torn newspaper. Then put colours on the walls with paint or crayon.

CONTINUED

- Next, using some card, make a stand up easel and table. Add other things such as the circular mirror by covering a circle of card with tinfoil. Make your own mini books and paint cans. You can personalise it by putting your own painting on the easel and adding objects you would like to have in your own studio.

TABLE DESIGN:
Card template

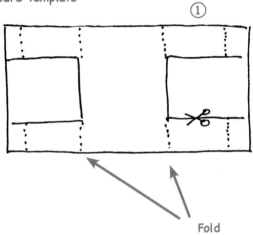

Fold

EASEL DESIGN:
Card template folded over

Fold here
Do not cut

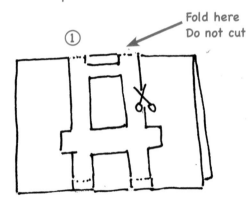

Table template assembled

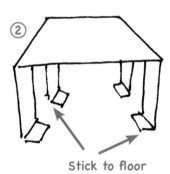

Stick to floor

Easel template assembled

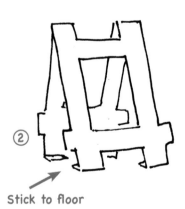

Stick to floor

- Cover the windows with light coloured clear plastic (optional). With the lid on, you can look at your studio through the windows and door or from above with the lid off.

Arttrivia

Auguste Renoir liked to keep an extremely tidy studio with everything kept clean and in order.

Drawing

The first mark on a blank page can be the most daunting and the most exciting!

Drawings and sketches have special qualities which make them very personal and informal. The speed with which sketches are made adds to their charm and informality. Sketches are generally small in scale and are made with the simplest of materials such as a pencil, piece of charcoal or pastel on paper. Because sketches are usually unfinished they can reveal the original ideas, thought processes and working methods of the artist. The very fact that sketches and drawings are 'unfinished' means they do not have to be perfect. They usually have a freshness and vitality that is sometimes lost in a finished painting.

Hugh Lane Reading by William Orpen

Sketches are sometimes observations made discreetly, capturing a glance or gesture without a person even being aware and without the 'stiffness' of a posed formal portrait. Drawings can also be very detailed studies valued as artworks in their own right or as important preparatory work for a finished painting.

Hugh Lane Reading by William Orpen

Hugh Lane and William Orpen were good friends as well as being distantly related and they travelled to France and Spain together in 1904. While in Paris, they visited the art dealer Durand-Ruel. It was from Durand-Ruel that Lane bought many of the great masterpieces of French art that were to form part of the Lane Bequest. William Orpen was widely admired for his skill in draughtsmanship or drawing and his precocious talent saw him enter the Metropolitan School of Art in Dublin shortly before his thirteenth birthday. The lovely sketch above shows Hugh Lane relaxing at home with his feet resting on the mantelpiece. During their travels together William Orpen observed that Lane would go to bed very late at night and get up late in the mornings. At the same time Hugh Lane was known for his energetic bursts of enthusiasm in the pursuit of getting things done.

Drawing of Francis Bacon's easel made during a Sunday Sketching workshop

For this reason Orpen's little sketch is additionally charming for revealing such an active character in a position of such repose.

Studies of an Irish
Wolfhound
by Briton Riviere

Studies of an Irish Wolfhound by Briton Riviere

Briton Riviere was one of the most famous and popular animal painters in Victorian Britain. Dogs, above all, appear throughout Riviere's work and they are often depicted in portraits of their masters. The dogs in his paintings were also used to suggest humour or sadness in the story being told and as an animal lover, he reveals them to live up to their reputation as man's best friend.

Unlike a still-life, it is not so easy to draw something that moves or fidgets a lot! However, the artist has revealed here how skilled he was at showing the wolfhound in different positions as well as the dog's alert expression and the softness of its fur.

Artists' Sketchbooks

Having a little pocket sketchbook and pencil ensures that you are always at the ready to record at a moment's notice an idea or an object that attracts your attention. Drawing encourages close observation and can stimulate fresh understanding of how paintings and sculptures are made. Drawing and sketching may also lead to discoveries of previously unnoticed details and also allows for lots of experimentation in your style and technique.

Art Activity

MAKING YOUR OWN ARTIST'S SKETCHBOOK

This little sketchbook is very easy to make and you can decorate the cover with your own design. You can add as many or as few pages as you like and can easily make new sketchbooks when your own one is full.

What you need:

For the sketchbook cover:

* 2 pieces of A5 size cardboard. The stiffer the cardboard, the more durable the sketchbook will be. Cardboard cut from an old box would be quite good.
* 4 coloured or plain pipe cleaners.
* Materials for decorating your sketchbook cover such as crayons, coloured paper, collage materials from old magazines, buttons, feathers, fabric, glitter.

For the inside pages:

* 6 A4 coloured or white sheets of paper (you can add additional sheets at this stage if you would like more pages in your sketchbook).
* Staples and stapler, glue, scissors.

Instructions:

* Carefully cut two pieces of A5 size cardboard. A5 is half of an A4 page. Some adult help may be needed when cutting the cardboard.

* Fold each of your A4 coloured paper sheets in half.

* Glue the folded A4 sheets together to create a concertina-style effect.

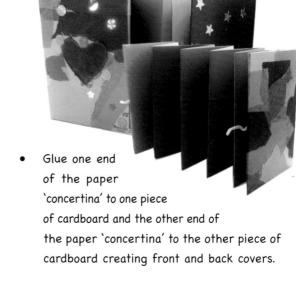

* Glue one end of the paper 'concertina' to one piece of cardboard and the other end of the paper 'concertina' to the other piece of cardboard creating front and back covers.

* To bind the covers, staple one side of each of the pipe cleaners to the cardboard covers and tie the other end of the pipe cleaners together.

* Decorating the cover of your book is as important as filling the sketchbook up with drawings, poems, observations and thoughts. Use the collage materials, glitter, feathers and other materials to help you decorate the front and back covers as you would like.

About Frames

As you walk through the gallery you will notice that nearly all the paintings, whatever their size, have a frame.

Some Impressionist painters such as **Pissarro** liked to use white frames because they looked bright. Also he felt the colour white would not compete with the colours in his paintings.

Most of these frames, particularly those surrounding paintings from the 19th and early 20th centuries, are very ornate and have a lot of decorative detail. These frames are sometimes made of wood but more often are made of plaster. As the floral and decorative detail is usually three-dimensional, these frames are prone to damage and need specialist care to repair and conserve them. Traditionally these frames were painted with a gold coloured pigment or skilfully covered in gold leaf. These are called gilded or gilt frames because of their colour. Frames surrounding paintings made more recently tend to be plainer and have little or no detail, although very plain frames were also fashionable a few hundred years ago.

Frame Detail. Like paintings or sculptures, frames are cleaned by specialist conservators.

As well as making a painting look finished, more ornate and showing it off to good advantage, a frame helps to protect a painting when it is on display, when it is being carried or when it is in storage. Occasionally paintings are also covered with a sheet of glass or perspex rather than being varnished. This may be because an artist liked the way the painting looked when glazed or because the layer of glass helps to protect thick impasto oil paint, for example with paintings by Jack B. Yeats. Varnishing an oil painting usually is sufficient to give the work a protective layer and a good finished appearance.

A frame generally matches the age and style of a painting although they are rarely made specifically for each other. Occasionally a frame may have been designed by the artist themselves, or by someone close to them, as in the case of *Un Matin* by William J.Leech.

Un Matin by William J. Leech

The timber frame surrounding William J. Leech's painting *Un Matin* is signed by the artist and has a delicate oriental inspired painted pattern.

More recently artists increasingly leave their work unframed, preferring to break with traditional means of showing art. Some artists like to let their paintings speak for themselves without any additional adornment or distractions.

The American artist **Mary Cassatt**, who exhibited with the French Impressionists, used both red and green frames.

Art Activity

MAKING AN ORNATE FRAME

Discover ornate detail in frames through sketching. Then use your drawing to help you make your own gold frame.

What you need:

Sketching materials:

* A4 paper
* Pencil
* Colouring pencils

Frame materials:

* A4 stiff card
* Light card
* Pencil
* Gold paint or yellow/orange/brown paint
* Glue
* Scissors
* Shells, dried flowers, leaves, gold spray paint (optional)

Instructions:

Step 1

* Start by looking at the gold frames around a number of the paintings in the gallery. Some of the larger frames are particularly ornate. If you look closely you will see many different patterns such as swirls, flowers and leaves.

* Choose a frame you like and study just one section - perhaps a corner. On an A4 page sketch that section of the frame exactly as you see it. At home use colouring pencils or paints to try and make your frame look gold. Yellow, orange and brown are all good colours for this. You could use blue and purple for the shadows.

Sketch of section of frame on A4 sheet

Painting

Corner of gold frame

Step 2

* To make a basic frame, cut a smaller rectangle out of the middle of your stiff A4 size card. Ask for adult help with this if you need to. The smaller rectangle that you cut out should be around the size of a postcard. Paint your frame in gold (or yellow/orange/brown) colour and leave to dry.

CONTINUED

Frame

A4

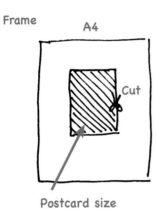

Cut

Postcard size

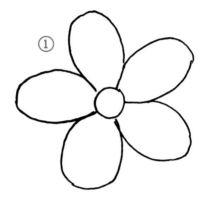

①

②

③

- On the lighter card draw some of the shapes you saw on the frames in the gallery such as flowers, leaves, circles, swirls. There are some templates here to help start you off.

- Cut out the shapes and paint them. When the shapes are dry, stick them to your frame. Arrange them so that they overlap and appear three-dimensional. Now all you need is a painting by you to make your very own Old Master!

Three-dimensional Frame:

- You could try sticking on real shells, dried flowers and leaves which have been covered with gold spray paint. Sticky tape, stronger glue and some adult help may be needed here.

Building Blocks of Art:
Colour, Tone & Texture

Homage to the Square
– Aglow
by Josef Albers

Why does an artist choose a particular colour or use brushstrokes in a certain way? The way these are used can dramatically change the way a painting looks.

COLOUR

Usually when you think of paintings you immediately think of colour. Artists use colour in very different ways. While some use colour to describe objects realistically, others use colour in an expressive way to give their painting a greater emotional strength. All colours have their own qualities. Some colours such as red and orange seem warm, while other colours such as blue or white can seem cold. Colours can also appear to change or glow if one colour is put beside another colour, for example when red is placed beside green. Colours are also associated with different emotions – red with anger or embarrassment, green with envy or sickness, yellow with cheerfulness or cowardice.

Homage to the Square – Aglow by Josef Albers
Josef Albers was fascinated by the way colours affect each other and how their appearance can seem to change when they are placed alongside another colour. Around 1950 Albers began a series which he called *Homage to the Square*. To pay homage to something is to praise it and hold it in high regard. Of all shapes, the square was his favourite. Through this series Albers experimented with different colour combinations using only the format of squares within squares. Albers would sometimes start with colour sketches which he would then develop into larger paintings or even tapestries. He eventually made over 1000 works

which explored colour harmony, and the illusion of colour coming forward or moving backwards. As well as naming each of his works *Homage to the Square*, he would sometimes add descriptions to his titles. For this painting he added the word 'Aglow'. The different orange tones of this painting placed beside each do seem to be warmly glowing and have a light of their own. In his series he combines squares, which are precise and mathematical shapes, with colour which is associated with emotion and whose appearance is changeable.

Garden Green
by Norah McGuinness

Garden Green is a still-life painting by the Irish artist Norah McGuinness. This painting is made up of lots of squares and is painted using mostly greens. On the table are a cup and saucer, a large black pot, two bottles, a spoon, a white cloth and a fruit and vegetable. But there is something strange about the way these objects appear. It looks as though they are sliding off the table! That is because the artist is painting in a Cubist style.

Cubism was a style of painting explored most famously by two artists – Picasso and Braque – in France at the beginning of the 20th century. Rather than paint from one direction, they showed objects from a number of different viewpoints – from the front, the side, the top, the

Garden Green
by Norah McGuinness

bottom and painted all these viewpoints together in the one painting. Rather than showing distance in a painting using perspective, the Cubists wanted to show how the surface of a painting is actually flat. In *Garden Green* it seems as though we are looking down on the spoon but looking across at the cup and saucer. If we were looking down at the cup and saucer we would be able to look right into it. Norah McGuinness has captured the sense of a lovely warm day. The kitchen table is before an open window with pink climbing roses outside. There is a girl in the garden. What do you think she is doing? Maybe she is picking something from the patchwork garden for dinner.

TONE

Tone is a word which describes the overall brightness or darkness of colours in a painting. Tone also describes shades of a similar colour. For example, a painting may be painted using mostly shades of dark to light grey and so could be described as having a grey tone or tonal range.

The Girl in White by Grace Henry

Grace Henry loved to use lots of bright colours when she painted the people of the west of Ireland. However, this painting of Miss Kitty Hearne is almost completely white except for Kitty's rosy cheeks and her dark hair and eyes.

The Girl in White
by Grace Henry

Wearing a lovely long white dress, Kitty seems to be daydreaming as she sits on a diamond patterned couch. While her dress is soft and flowing the rest of the painting, such as the wood panelling behind her head, is made up of strong geometric shapes. The combination of using mostly the colour white with such clear patterns makes the painting appear flat and delicate.

TEXTURE

The way paint is applied, whether thickly or thinly, or the addition of materials such as sand, can change the appearance and expressive quality of a painting dramatically. William Orpen's still-life objects in *Reflections: China and Japan* look amazingly shiny and real. Orpen used very diluted, thinly applied paint to help him achieve this effect.

Reflections: China and Japan
by William Orpen

In contrast, *There is No Night* by Jack B. Yeats is a celebration of texture and *impasto* oil painting. *Impasto* is a word to describe thickly applied oil paint. Yeats uses lots of oil paint and expressive, colourful brushstrokes which makes the surface of his painting bumpy and raised. All this raised texture is only emphasised further by the parts of his painting where he has left the canvas almost bare.

There is No Night
by Jack B. Yeats

Art Activity

TONAL STORIES

What you need:

* Various coloured papers from a paper pack or torn from old magazines.
* You could also use coloured fabrics or coloured tissue paper. The more variation in colour and texture the better.
* Scissors
* White paper
* Pencils
* Pritt stick glue

Instructions:

* Lay out lots of different coloured paper or fabric in piles of similar colour e.g. all green tones together, all pinks and reds together and so on.

* Pick a colour to work with and collect a bundle from your chosen colour.

* On a white sheet of paper arrange your chosen colour from darkest tone to lightest in bands across the page. You can cut neat stripes or tear strips for a more varied effect. The end result will generally look like thick or thin stripes of colour with scissor cut or torn edges.

* When your page is completely covered in colour, ask yourself what you think the arrangement of coloured stripes reminds

you of. For example, a page of greens often resembles hills and fields in the countryside or stripes of pinks can look like a pile of mattresses. This idea will form the basis for a page from your story.

* When you have chosen an image, cut out shapes in plain paper which tell your story – perhaps cutting out clouds to float across the green stripes will make a landscape, or a camel on yellow tonal bands of colour which had looked like a desert. Stick these shapes onto your tonal stripes.

* If making this in your classroom, tell your tonal stories in full to each other or at home to your family.

Art Activity

PAINTING MULTI-COLOURED BUTTERFLIES

What you need:
* A3 white paper
* Pencils
* Poster paint and paint brushes
* Paint trays or old plate to mix your colours
* PVA glue
* Glitter, sequins and eyeballs (optional)

Instructions:
* During a visit to the gallery, look at the many colours and patterns you see in the paintings around you as inspiration for your imaginary multi-coloured butterflies. You could also look at some nature books to find out more about butterfly shapes and colours or keep a close eye out for fluttering butterflies in your garden or in the local park.

* With your pencil, fill your A3 paper with your butterfly design. There is a line drawing here to help you with the shape. Fill your butterfly wings with lots of patterns, swirls, spirals, dots, circles and stripes.

* Next paint your butterfly. You could mix different colours together to create new colours. For example, mix red and blue to get purple or place light colours beside dark colours to see how each enhances the vibrancy of the other.

* When the butterfly is fully painted then add textured decorations by glueing on sequins or glitter. Finally place two eyeballs on the head for a 3D effect. This is optional and the butterfly will look just as great with painted eyes.

* When the butterfly is finished you could fill in the background of your picture with flowers or long grass.

BUTTERFLY LINE DRAWING

Art Activity

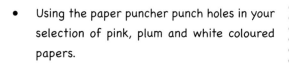

CHERRY BLOSSOMS

This art activity makes a very light and delicate Japanese inspired artwork.

What you need:

* White, pink and plum coloured paper (Note: tissue paper is too delicate for this and sugar paper or cartridge paper would work better).
* A paper puncher
* Masking tape
* Pritt stick glue
* Brown oil pastel

Instructions:

- Take a sheet of a light coloured paper as the background

- Then tear pieces of masking tape of various lengths. Twist these lengths randomly so that the tape takes on a loose texture to look like tree bark and branches. Colour these twisted lengths of masking tape with brown oil pastel. Then stick them to the background sheet of paper in the shape of a tree.

- Using the paper puncher punch holes in your selection of pink, plum and white coloured papers.

- Having carefully put glue on your twisted bark and branches, you could randomly sprinkle them with your dots of colour for a blossom cloud effect, or in groups of five dots to create petal clusters.

Art and Music

Above:
Music in the Tuileries
Gardens
(La Musique aux Tuileries)
by Edouard Manet
with detail below

Composition, theme, rhythm, colour, tone, texture and harmony are all terms that are used to describe both art and music. Wouldn't it be great if some of the people you see in paintings could talk? We could listen to their stories and ask them lots of questions. It is up to our vivid imaginations to wonder about the tunes and melodies that are being played and sung in the paintings here.

Music in the Tuileries Gardens by Edouard Manet

Music in the Tuileries Gardens shows some of Manet's fashionably dressed family and friends gathered to enjoy an afternoon concert in Paris. The more you look at this painting the more you discover: in the centre two small children are playing with buckets while to the side some toys – a hula hoop and ball – are lying beside a chair. You can also just see a little boy in a hat peeking out from behind a woman's shoulder.

Rather than painting the musicians, this painting is a spectacular group portrait. Some of the people shown in the painting were well known: they include the poet and critic Charles Baudelaire, the composer Jacques Offenbach and the painter Henri Fantin-Latour. The artist's brother, Eugène Manet, who was married to the Impressionist painter Berthe Morisot, is also shown in the painting.

When this painting was first shown in 1863 not everybody liked the way Manet painted the array of hats in careful detail while he painted other parts, including some of the faces, with loose and blurry brushstrokes. Others were astounded by the strong contrasts between light and dark colours. The fact that he shows everyday Parisian life in a known outdoor setting, rather than a biblical, mythological or historical story was also shocking to some. However, many were excited by Manet's painting for all these very reasons.

The Accordion Player by Jack B. Yeats

The Accordion Player is a watercolour by the great Irish artist Jack B. Yeats. Jack B. Yeats travelled around Ireland and he loved making drawings and sketches of the characters he met. This accordion player is sitting on a simple wooden bench and is tapping his foot on the floor to the rhythm of the music. The only person listening seems to be a man standing in the doorway. Perhaps he was in the other room and heard the accordion player play a tune that he liked and decided to come in and listen. The room is very bare except for a painting on the wall. This painting is of a girl in a Spanish-type dress and it is called 'The Belle of the Pacific.' Maybe these men are old sailors and the accordion player is playing a tune that reminds them of their travels abroad and on the high seas.

The Accordion Player
by Jack B. Yeats

Cellomaster
by Arman

Cellomaster by Arman

Arman once said that musical instruments fascinated him. One of the reasons he liked cellos, for instance, was that his father played the cello. He also liked the beautiful curved shape of cellos. Here in *Cellomaster* you can see the ornate carved head of the cello with four tuning pegs. The f-holes on the side of the cello let the sound out. Unlike this bronze sculpture, cellos are normally made of wood and the bow would be of horsehair. *Cellomaster* is also very unusual because of its jagged shape. It looks as though the cello has been cut into horizontal pieces and sort of put back together. Arman thought you could find out more about an instrument by looking at it in sections and then, like a jigsaw, by putting it back together again. Each piece of *Cellomaster* is like a step. You could imagine that each step is a note in a musical scale (do, re, mi, fa, so, la, ti, do). The cello also looks like it is vibrating from a musical note that has just been played.

The Street Singer by Jerome Connor

Even though this sculpture is made of cold bronze, it still appears quite lifelike. The street singer is staring into the distance and seems to be carried away by her song. You can really imagine that she is singing by the way the artist has shown her with her mouth open. She is wearing a scarf over her head, perhaps because it is cold and she wants to keep warm. What type of song do you think this street singer is singing? Have you heard any buskers recently when you were in town?

The Street Singer
by Jerome Connor

Art Activity

ART AND MUSIC IDEAS

∗ Experiment like Arman's Cellomaster and make a drawing of an instrument's separate parts. Draw a new instrument by assembling these separate parts in a new way.

∗ Imagine you are the street singer or one of the characters in The Accordion Player. Write a short story or poem about yourself and your music.

∗ Make abstract drawings to the sound of music – what colours, shapes and lines do you imagine when you hear a particular piece of music?

∗ Make your own 'street singer' with modelling clay.

∗ Look at other artists who have been inspired by music and instruments. The artist Pablo Picasso painted and made collages of guitars while Wassily Kandinsky was fascinated by musical and colour harmonies.

COMPOSE A MUSICAL PIECE INSPIRED BY PAINTINGS AND SCULPTURES

During Art and Music workshops for children at the gallery we explore paintings and sculpture by first looking at a painting or sculpture. Bold or delicate brushstrokes, patterns, rhythm, texture, shapes and colours as well as the story that is being told can all spark ideas. Then a simple piece is composed and performed by children using basic, though evocative, musical and percussion instruments such as 'rainmakers', triangles, tambourines, bongos and rhythm sticks. The puddles and rain drops of Les Parapluies by Renoir, the mysteriousness of Boulevard Raspail by Roderic O'Conor and the hectic streetscape of Boulevard de Clichy by Bonnard have all inspired mini-masterpieces!

Following the Artists' Animal Trail

Animals of different shapes, sizes and species have inspired artists for centuries. The collection of Dublin City Gallery The Hugh Lane has many paintings and sculptures of animals. Even the building in which the gallery is housed has ornate animal motifs in the decorative plasterwork as well as lion head handles at the front door.

Big Bird by Niki de Saint Phalle

Big Bird was made by Niki de Saint Phalle, an artist whose work is an explosion of life and colour. Big Bird, who looks as though he lives in a tropical rain forest, is full of personality and playfulness. He is made of brightly painted plaster and has several holes through which you can look so you can see the sky, or plants or the gallery space around you. Niki de Saint Phalle described this type of work as an 'air sculpture'. The coiled lead looks like it is unravelling and *Big Bird* is about to fly away!

Birds were very symbolic for Niki de Saint Phalle and they occur frequently throughout her work. She also made fantastic creatures and monsters inspired by her imagination. Many of these very large and colourful works were made for specially designed sculpture gardens and outdoor areas for children.

Big Bird
by Niki de
Saint Phalle

Thoroughbred Horse Walking by Edgar Degas

Thoroughbred Horse Walking is by the French artist Edgar Degas. Degas loved going to the races and he made lots of sketches of horses and jockeys. He also made sculptures of horses in various stages of motion, such as horses walking, trotting or jumping. In the 19th century photography had just been

Thoroughbred
Horse Walking
by Edgar Degas

Leaf torn from
Animals in Motion
(1901) by Eadweard
Muybridge,
showing a series of
photographs of a
dog running. This
page was found
in Francis Bacon's
Studio.

invented. Degas had a little box camera which he used to take photographs at the racecourse. The photographic stills taken by Eadweard Muybridge were of immense interest to Degas as they showed clearly how a horse moved. Degas's little horse was originally modelled in wax and supported by wire. You can see some of this wire at the neck and along the spine of the horse. In the gallery, if you look closely you will see a finger print on the horse's belly. The wax sculpture was later cast in bronze after Degas's death. Movement was an important theme in Degas's art. Ballet dancers were also among his favourite subjects and they share the grace and suppleness of the thoroughbred horse.

Shark Lady in a Balldress by Dorothy Cross

Shark Lady in a Balldress by Dorothy Cross is a wonderful sculpture made with great skill. Sharks have a fearsome reputation and we normally do not associate them with going to dances! However, this shark lady is wearing a magnificent glittering gown of golden brown. The shark lady's body, her breasts and fin, are made of polished bronze while the skirt is made of delicate woven bronze. Can you think of other sea creatures who may be going to this imaginary ball under the sea?

Shark Lady in a Balldress
by Dorothy Cross

Monkey and Dog
by John Kindness

Monkey and Dog by John Kindness

John Kindness uses pieces of mosaic of contrasting colours for his sculpture *Monkey and Dog*. The monkey is vivid blue while the dog is red. There is a great sense of movement and ferocity in *Monkey and Dog*. This is helped by the brightly coloured patterns the artist has used such as stars or lozenges which seem to pulsate. The circular, ball-like shape of the sculpture, inspired by Japanese *netsuke*, also helps achieve this sense of movement. The animals here are used in a symbolic way as this work was inspired by political events in Northern Ireland and the stubborn and often violent defence of tradition. Walk around this work and look at it from different angles. Sometimes it seems that the monkey is attacking the poor dog and other times that the dog is attacking the poor monkey. Both, however, are chasing each other.

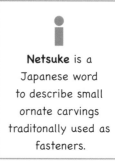

Netsuke is a Japanese word to describe small ornate carvings traditonally used as fasteners.

Lion's Head Door Knocker

The Lion's Head door knockers at the front entrance to the gallery are one of a number of decorative features of Charlemont House, the 18th century house in which part of the gallery is housed. What animal would you choose to put at your front door? Why would you choose this animal?

Lion's Head door knocker at the entrance to the gallery

The Travelling Circus
by Jack B. Yeats

The Travelling Circus by Jack B. Yeats

Growing up in Co. Sligo, the talented and curious Jack B. Yeats found fishermen, circuses, horse races and fair days a rich source of inspiration. His father and sisters were also artistic while his brother was the famous poet William Butler Yeats.

The Travelling Circus is an early **watercolour** which may have been painted by Jack B. Yeats out of doors as he watched the circus being set up. This watercolour is full of amazing details such as the crowd of people queuing to get into the Big Top where they are welcomed by a man in a Chinese outfit; the man carrying meat to feed the tiger on the right hand side of the drawing; and the clowns entertaining a group of children to the side of the Big Top. See also how the Ring Master in his top hat is telling the crowd to step back as the dappled horses are being led through. Notice also how everyone is wearing a hat or a cap as this was the fashion of the day.

Have you ever been to a circus? What is your favourite thing about the circus? Maybe it is the clowns, the acrobats, the skill of the animals, the lights and atmosphere, or the excitement of the circus coming to town?

> **Watercolour** is a thin type of paint which is diluted with water and is usually used on paper or cardboard.

Art Activity

AROUND THE WORLD WITH BIG BIRD!

Why not find out more about some of the wonderful animals from around the globe and closer to home? Choose an animal that inspires you – perhaps the cheekiness and agility of a monkey, the majesty of an elephant or the exotic plumage of a cockatoo! Find out as much as you can about your chosen animal – what it looks like, what it likes to eat, what it sounds like, where it lives. Pin point the location of your animal's habitat on a world map.

Make a painting or small clay model of your chosen animal and paint the clay in the animal's colours. You could also make a painted or collage desert or jungle habitat backdrop in a three-sided cardboard box.

A clay mandril made during art workshops with Gaelscoil Coláiste Mhuire.

Biblical Stories, Fairytales & Legends

Adam and Eve
in the Garden
by Louis le Brocquy

Biblical stories, fairytales and legends have provided artists with rich sources of inspiration and stirred their imaginations. Which part of the story do they choose and how do they tell it? The same scene could be shown by a number of artists in very different ways.

Adam and Eve in the Garden by Louis le Brocquy

Louis le Brocquy is an artist who is continually exploring and experimenting with new subject matter and media. As a young man he was greatly inspired by the old master paintings of Velázquez and Goya as well as by more recent masters of modern art such as Degas, Manet, Cézanne and Picasso. In the late 1940's and early 1950's, le Brocquy was introduced to, or as he said 'stumbled on by accident', the medium of tapestry. Tapestry – as fabric wall hangings – belongs to an age old tradition and le Brocquy collaborated with the Tabard workshop at Aubusson in France in the making of his. In 1951, le Brocquy was asked to design tapestries on the biblical theme of Adam and Eve from the Old Testament. Le Brocquy has cleverly arranged his story as a frieze divided into three parts. Here we see Eve,

A **symbol** is something which stands for a person, a characteristic, a place or an object without describing them exactly.
Symbols used by le Brocquy in Adam and Eve include the moon as a symbol for the female Eve, and the sun as a symbol for the male Adam.

encouraged by the evil snake, tempting Adam with an apple from the Tree of Knowledge. Because they were specifically forbidden to taste fruit from this tree, both Adam and Eve were expelled from the Garden of Eden. At the centre of the tapestry, le Brocquy's Tree of Knowledge is full of little birds and butterflies as well as more unusual symbols such as flying fish and eyes!

Cinderella Dressing Her Ugly Sister by Wilhelmina Geddes

This watercolour is an early work by Wilhelmina Geddes and shows Cinderella helping one of the ugly sisters to get ready for the ball. Wearing a bright yellow balldress and sitting at her dressing table, the ugly sister is admiring a ribbon which Cinderella will tie in her hair. Cinderella is shown here wearing a hair cap and in her dull working clothes before she was dramatically transformed by the Fairy Godmother. Cinderella was modelled on Florence, the youngest sister of the artist. Wilhelmina Geddes later went on to become an accomplished stained glass artist.

Cinderella Dressing her Ugly Sister by Wilhelmina Geddes

The Eve of Saint Agnes by Harry Clarke

Harry Clarke originally made this magnificent stained glass window of *The Eve of Saint Agnes* for a house in Ailesbury Road in Dublin. The theme was inspired by a poem of the same name written by the English poet John Keats (1795-1817). Using colourful, intricate detail Harry Clarke has etched onto glass the dramatic escape of Porphyro and Madeline. The young couple were forbidden to marry by Madeline's father Sir Maurice. Harry Clarke tells the story by dividing it into fourteen glass panels. Beneath these is a frieze showing the different characters in the story. The costumes of each of the characters, with their ornate patterns and colours, are amazingly imaginative and decorative.

Traditionally on 20th January, the eve of the feast of St. Agnes, young girls would dream of their future husbands.

The Eve of Saint Agnes
by Harry Clarke

This stained glass window tells the story of a young man and woman who fell in love but were forbidden to marry.

?

Who is this fantastical creature and where did he come from?

What wonderful adventure are they on? To what far off place are they travelling?

The Winged Horse
by George Russell

The Winged Horse by George Russell

As well as being a painter, George Russell was a writer, a philosopher and a poet. He was an inventive person who was very sensitive to the mystical and spiritual possibilities of the everyday world around him. This painting shows a boy riding a winged horse over the ocean waves. Both are bathed in golden light and rays of sunlight radiate from the boy's head like a crown. Russell, who was also known as AE, expressed his imaginative ideas through his painting and the curving brushstrokes give a great sense of emotion to this work.

The Sleeping Princess by Edward Burne-Jones

The English artist Burne-Jones was fascinated by the legend of Briar Rose and he made several paintings inspired by this theme. The legend is similar to that of Sleeping Beauty, who pricked her finger on a spinning wheel causing the entire kingdom, including the King and Queen, the cooks, the blacksmiths and the servants, to fall asleep for one hundred years.

If you look closely at this painting you will notice that there is no spinning wheel. Instead, Princess Briar Rose may have accidentally pricked her finger on a thorn while admiring the lovely pink climbing roses. Burne-Jones has shown the Princess

i

Burne-Jones loved painting in meticulous detail and in this painting he has taken great care with painting each leaf, petal, the folds of the dresses, and the grain of the timber floor.

The Sleeping Princess
by Edward Burne-Jones

asleep with some of her ladies-in-waiting, one of whom has a stringed instrument lying by her side. Unlike everything else throughout the kingdom, Nature did not fall asleep. The trees and flowers in the forest kept on growing and here the roses have entwined themselves around everyone as they sleep. Something else in the painting shows that time is passing. At the very right hand side of the painting is a tall object. While it looks like a lamp it is in fact an hourglass with sand in it.

Burne-Jones painted another version of The Sleeping Princess which is very similar to the one in this gallery except that the Princess and her friends have more colourful clothes and there is a jewelled crown and mirror lying on the ground.

Art Activity

Why not draw a different stage of the story of the Sleeping Princess? You could show the Princess when she was very young, or the rest of the kingdom asleep or perhaps the Prince battling his way through the forest and breaking the spell with a kiss!

Art Activity

MAKING A FAIRYTALE STAINED GLASS BANNER

What you need:

✳ Tracing paper

✳ Coloured cellophane paper

✳ Coloured tissue paper

✳ Glitter

✳ Glue and scissors.

Instructions:

• The best way to start this activity is to think of what stained glass looks like. It is transparent and colourful. We often see it used in churches, telling us religious stories. In Harry Clarke's window The Eve of St Agnes he also tells a story. It is about a young man and woman who fall in love. He uses beautiful clear colours, lots of purples, blues, pinks and yellows, but also he has carefully planned how to tell his story in pictures.

• To make your fairytale stained glass banner you too will have to think about this. First pick your favourite fairytale, think of Rapunzel, Sleeping Beauty or Cinderella. Then pick out the most important events in the story. This will help you plan how you will make your banner.

• Once you have decided on your story in pictures, sketch out your images onto a big sheet of tracing paper. If you are really adventurous or there are a few of you making it, maybe stick three pieces of A1 size tracing paper together, remembering that it will have to fit on a window. If there is not a window that will fit a banner this size, maybe make three separate banners, each one telling a different phase of your story.

• Once you have sketched out your story you can start cutting out pieces of cellophane paper and sticking it on. Cellophane paper is completely see through but comes in lots of different colours, so it gives a very similar effect as stained glass. Cutting out sections and shapes of tissue paper will also give the effect of stained glass. By layering on your different papers, for example placing cellophane over tissue paper, you can make your stained glass look richer.

• When you have completed your fairytale in pictures, stick it to a really large window. Then you will see the light from outside flood through your banner, lighting up the story you have told.

Artists and the Great Outdoors

Nature and the changing seasons offer constant inspiration to writers, poets, musicians and artists. In the gallery you will see how artists have captured the warmth of a sunny beach, the hustle and bustle of a rainy day or the force of wind on a blustery headland. In fact during your visit you could nearly see all the seasons in one day!

Summer's Day (Jour d'Été) by Berthe Morisot

Summer is a great time of the year especially if you are an artist who likes to paint out of doors! *Jour d'Été* is a beautiful painting by the French artist Berthe Morisot. *Jour d'Été* means 'summer's day' in French. This painting shows two women boating on a lake in the Bois de Boulogne, a large park in Paris. One of the women is looking at a group of ducks that are swimming close to the boat. Berthe Morisot was one of the most successful Impressionist painters, a group of artists who loved to paint out of doors. Her zig zag brushstrokes shows how quickly she painted. Why do you think she would have to paint quickly?

Summer's Day
(Jour d'Été)
by Berthe Morisot

Sutton Courtenay
(Summer on the River)
by John Lavery
with detail below

Sutton Courtenay (Summer on the River) by John Lavery

Summer on the River was painted by John Lavery and shows a very fashionably dressed man and three women enjoying a lazy summer's day on a river in Edwardian England. The woman in the green hat looks as though she is reading her book or maybe she is drawing. Another woman whom we cannot see is sheltering under her red parasol or sun umbrella. Their names were Violet and Elizabeth. The little dog sitting on the bow of the punt was called Pompey. The man and woman on the other punt may have sailed close by to say hello. Maybe it is a very hot day and, like the others, they are sheltering under the shade of a tree by the riverbank. Two swans are looking over. Perhaps they are hoping for some scraps left over from a picnic!

66 *Anything painted directly from nature and on the spot has always a force, power and vivacity of touch that one cannot find in the studio* 99

Eugene Boudin

At the Seaside by Eugene Boudin with detail below

At the Seaside by Eugene Boudin

Eugene Boudin painted *At the Seaside* in 1867. *At the Seaside* shows the clothes fashionable at that time. The women are wearing long dresses with full petticoats and on their heads are hats with ribbons. It is a very blustery day and their ribbons are being blown in the air. Going to the seaside was a very sociable event and some among the large crowd of people have brought chairs to sit on while others are standing around chatting with each other. In the background are white tents where people would change into their swimming costumes. The swimming costumes of 1867 were not like those you would see today. The man on the left hand side of the painting, clinging to a robe over his head, is wearing togs that are almost full length and go down to his knees. In the background are other swimmers in the sea but the sky looks overcast and the water quite chilly!

Boy on Shore
by Walter Osborne

Boy on Shore by Walter Osborne

The Irish artist Walter Osborne painted *Boy on Shore*. This is a very small oil painting showing a young boy day dreaming on a sunny beach. Walter Osborne painted in France, England and Ireland and he was particularly fond of artists such as Edgar Degas and Claude Monet. Like Eugene Boudin, Osborne loved to paint outside in the fresh air. Even though this is such a small painting, you can almost feel the warmth of the sunshine. The boy's face is in the shade while the strong sunlight shines on the back of his white top. Osborne has used sketch-like brushstrokes of warm colours like red, orange and yellow to paint the soft golden sand.

The horizon line – where the sea meets the sky – is at the very top of this painting.

Beach Scene, South of France by William J. Leech

Beach Scene, South of France was painted by the Irish artist William J. Leech. Leech was a pupil of the artist Walter Osborne and he said on many occasions that of all the schools he attended, Walter Osborne was the best teacher he ever had. Leech painted this work while in the South of France between 1921-26, and you can see how fashions have changed since Boudin painted *At the Seaside*. Two women are strolling along barefoot on the beach with one looking directly at us. They both have colourful parasols to shade their faces. When Leech painted this work it was not fashionable for people to have a suntan. Leech is famous for his colourful brushstrokes and you can see this in the bright red headscarf of the woman with the pink parasol. In the background are children playing in the water: two boys in striped tops are jumping from a rock into the cool water. At the other side are two little girls with matching green sun hats paddling in the water. Leech has used stripes of colours such as purple, turquoise and green to show the lapping waves. The shadows of the two women are also painted in blue and turquoise rather than black.

Beach Scene,
South of France
by William J. Leech

Art Activity

AUTUMN FALLING LEAVES

What you need:

* Sugar paper, tissue paper
* Crepe paper in different colours
* Glue and scissors
* Glitter and sequins
* String in different colours

Instructions:

* Taking inspiration from a walk in a leafy park during autumn, remember the feeling of crunchy red and orange leaves under your feet. Remember how leaves fall from the trees spiralling down to the ground. It is also a good opportunity to look at the shapes of leaves from different kinds of trees.

* To begin, gather a variety of papers (crepe, tissue, sugar paper and even hand made papers) all with different textures and translucency. The colours of these papers should be warm and autumnal – reds, pinks, browns, yellows, oranges. Also different materials like lace and tulle can be used to show the delicate quality of autumn leaves.

* Begin to cut out different shaped leaves, as though you had found them in a forest full of chestnut, oak and beech trees. You can roughly sketch out the shapes of different leaf types and use these as a template for all your leaves or you can make leaves that are of all different shapes and sizes. When

you have between fifteen and twenty leaves you can begin to decorate them.

* To decorate your leaves you can use scraps of coloured paper, like a collage, layering different colours and papers to create the texture of a leaf. You can also use glitter and colourful sequins to make your leaves magical, as though the light has just caught them through the branches of the trees above.

This Summer Tree installation was made by children and families at the gallery with artist Sinéad McGeeney.

* When you have finished decorating your leaves, gather them all together. Use some string which matches your leaves, maybe it has gold running through it or is bright red or orange. Attach a length of string to the end of each of your leaves. Then gather each length of string and tie them all together. Now you have a whole bundle of autumn leaves that can billow in the wind but never blow away. You can run with them in the park or you can hang them from the ceiling in your room, like a mobile, and watch them twirl as you fall asleep.

The Diligence in
the Snow
by Gustave Courbet
with detail below

The Diligence in the Snow by Gustave Courbet

The Diligence in the Snow is a very large painting by the French artist Gustave Courbet and shows a huge snowdrift covering the landscape. So much of the painting is covered in white, you can almost feel the cold. To one side there are farmhouses and looming in the distance are large grey clouds. A carriage pulled by oxen and horses is stuck in the snow. Some people, perhaps the passengers and local farmers, are trying to help the struggling animals and overturned coach. If you look closely you can see someone sitting on one of the oxen. His hands are pulled inside his coat and held close to his body for warmth.

Diligence is the French word for a stagecoach which brought people from place to place before cars, trains or buses.

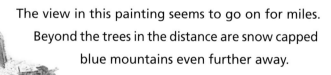

The view in this painting seems to go on for miles. Beyond the trees in the distance are snow capped blue mountains even further away.

Lavacourt Under Snow
by Claude Monet

Lavacourt Under Snow by Claude Monet

The French Impressionist artist Claude Monet loved painting in the open air. He would often paint the same scene over and over again just to see how it looked at different times of the day, at different times of the year and under different weather conditions.

This painting shows the village of Lavacourt under a blanket of snow. The snow is a blue colour perhaps because it is either early morning or evening is approaching. In the distance, the sun is shining on the pale pink hills. Blue is a cool colour and really shows how cold the snow is. To the left of the painting is the River Seine with two boats moored at the riverbank. Can you see all the thick brushstrokes of different colours that Monet liked to use? When painting outside, he would usually have had to paint quite quickly, particularly if it was chilly!

The Impressionists avoided using the colour black to show shadows. Like other artists at that time, Monet availed of the huge range of newly developed colour pigments. One of these was **cobalt blue** which he used in this painting.

Skating in Holland
by an Imitator of Johan Jongkind

Skating in Holland by an Imitator of Johan Jongkind

School of means
in the style of
a particular
artist though not
necessarily painted
by the artist.

This painting is full of the light of a setting sun on a cold winter's day. Jongkind was fascinated by the fleeting effects of light and you can see in this painting how the light bounces off the ice and snow covered fields. The figures gliding along on their iceskates are like silhouettes against the golden sunset. Even though the light is fading with the short winter day, there are many people out enjoying themselves on the frozen river. In the background are windmills, showing this to be Holland, the country where Jongkind was born. While Jongkind painted many scenes similar to *Skating in Holland*, this particular work is thought to have been painted by someone imitating or copying his composition and style.

Art Activity

WINTER BONNETS

What you need:
* Sugar paper
* Crepe paper
* Tissue paper
* Scissors and sellotape

To decorate your bonnet:
* Glitter, sequins, icicle streamers, tinsel, cotton wool (optional)

Instructions:

* For this art activity, we are going to make winter bonnets. Celebrate the chilly season by looking at rain drops, snow flakes, deep black clouds and blowing winds. We will keep to cold colours like blue, grey, white, black, and silver for the background colour of our bonnets. These colours will make us feel like there is a nip in the air outside.

* It is a good idea to look at different kind of hats before you start to get some ideas. The milliner Philip Treacy makes really exciting and exotic hats. A lovely painting by John Lavery called Japanese Switzerland, shows Lady Lavery and her daughter Alice wearing very elegant hats. They are to keep them warm in the cold weather but are also very stylish.

* To make the basic shape for your bonnet take an A3 piece of grey sugar paper, fold it in half, and then quarter it (fig.1). Making sure you have the folded corner or centre facing away from you, cut the other two corners away in a curve (see fig.2) to create the shape for your bonnet.

* Then we cut out one of the folded sections (see fig.3). Once this is done, take both sides and pinch them together, creating a cone shape (fig.4). Once you have this cone shape in place, sellotape the two sides together.

* Decorate your bonnet with glitter, sparkly

fig.1    fig.2

fig.3    fig.4

Creating the winter bonnets

sequins, or winter inspired cotton snow balls, icicle streamers, tinsel or paper snowflakes.

* You could also draw winter inspired scenes and decorations onto the A3 sugar paper before you fold it.

Poetry and Art

When the poet Enda Wyley was a little girl she made a visit to Dublin City Gallery The Hugh Lane or The Municipal Gallery as it was then known. Here she recalls her visit and the huge impression the painting *Large Solar Device* by Patrick Scott had on her as a child.

Poet Enda Wyley

"It is Sunday, my favourite day of the week and I am nine years old again. I am clambering up Killiney Hill with my brothers and sisters. Later, we go with our mum and dad to feed the ducks in Herbert Park. But we know that the real treat of the day will be when we reach the top of Parnell Square, the city spread out below us. For there, elegant above the Garden of Remembrance, stands the Hugh Lane Gallery. Of all our Sunday adventures, this is our favourite one. We love to visit the majestic house – love its wooden floors and high windows. But most of all we love all the paintings and the stories that they tell.

My sister wants to be the little girl in Renoir's Les Parapluies, her umbrella raised above her pretty soft-hatted face. My brother is transfixed by Maude Gonne, tall and handsome, holding a monkey in Sarah Purser's painting of her in a puff-sleeved, old fashioned dress.

I like all these paintings too – but my favourite is a huge orange ball, paint trickling down the canvas. It is an explosion of colour creeping into my head and heart. A man called Patrick Scott made it and it is to this beautiful painting that I run breathless on this Sunday afternoon, leaving my parents and siblings far behind.

Later, back at home in our kitchen, I get out my old paint box and with a straw try to blow reds and yellows and orange onto a big piece of paper on the floor. I badly want to make my own big sun, like the one in the gallery. It looked so simple, so easy in the gallery. But, crouched on our blue floor tiles, I soon find out just how hard it is to make a powerful orange ball with paint. I make up my mind that this man Patrick Scott, must be a very magical man, full of tricks and secrets. After all, he knows how to change paint into a wonderful thing."

"Now I am older, I know that words like paintings can tell a story too in their own way. On a visit to the Hugh Lane Gallery I seek out the Patrick Scott painting I so loved as a child and immediately feel my heart miss a beat when I see it again. It is like meeting an old friend.

I sit on a cushioned bench and begin to scribble on the back of an old envelope about just how the Big Solar Device made me so happy when I was a little girl and loved to stare at it. The words flow and flow. And suddenly an idea dawns on me. It is in childhood that the best poems begin."

Enda Wyley, 2006

Art Activity

POETRY AND ART IDEAS

* **Write a Story**

    Paintings, like poems, can tell a story. Choose a painting or a piece of art in the gallery that you really like. Imagine you are in the painting. What does it feel like? What is happening? Write a story about who and where you are.

* **Blow Painting**

    Using paints, mix red and yellow to make orange. Try painting a huge sun on a large piece of paper. Using your brush, let paint trickle down from the sun or with a straw blow paint on it to create an effect like the one in Patrick Scott's painting.

* **Word Sun**

    Sit in front of Patrick Scott's painting Large Solar Device. Look and look at it. Feel the heat of the colours. Look at the way the paint trickles down the canvas.

    Write a list of words it makes you think of – for example volcano, fire, Easter sun. Cut a large piece of paper into a circle and paint it a bright orange colour. Cut other pieces into the shape of sunrays. Write your new words on these rays. Glue the sun with the rays bursting from it on a larger piece of black paper. You have made a word sun to hang on your wall!

    ● W.B. Yeats wrote several poems about this gallery, including "The Municipal Gallery Revisited."

Municipal Gallery Favourite
(After Patrick Scott)

I want to blow again
down the fine straw
of my childhood days
that sunburst -
huge orange gasp
splattered on the canvas.

It was our favourite painting,
magic as penny wishes
below the winged Children of Lir
in the Garden of Remembrance,
necessary as stale bread in paper bags
for the ducks in Herbert Park,
beautiful as the kite-high view
of Killiney Bay
we clambered for up Victoria Hill.

Too bored by dull attendants,
pompous guides, or parents,
we spun many races each week,
dared one another
to whizz shouting down
the great bannister slide
and leap again
up the marble stairs;

then loved to burst
with our bare feet
tar bubbles on the summer roads,
loved tree swings
over secret backyard jungles,
the ivy huts we hid in,

woven across orchard walls - but more,
this orange, paint-blown shape
that made our church clothes casual,
our thoughts simple, arrogant
on Sunday visits,
"Bet we could do that too
if we'd paper big enough!"

Now I stroll the gallery with you
during holy hours.
A man is talking about a painting.
I stop and join the intent group.
Afterwards I find
A cushioned bench to rest on.

Somewhere below
I know the sunburst favourite
is dulled by basement dust
and lack of funds;
I try to catch its light again
in another piece near by -

a grey figure stumbles
along a white strand curve,
while behind mountains
only tips of gold
suggest a fallen warmth.

Enda Wyley

This is the poem written by Enda many years later, inspired by Patrick Scott's painting.

Large Solar Device was painted by the Irish artist Patrick Scott. It belongs to a series of paintings painted by him that were inspired by the testing of nuclear weapons in the 1960's. This painting reveals the artist's horrified reaction to such massively destructive weapons. It also shows the dramatic and strange beauty of such explosions represented here by the glowing sphere. The sphere became a powerful recurring idea in Scott's paintings from this time.

Looking at 3D Works of Art

Sculptures and 3D works of art can be made in many ways depending on what materials the artist is using and how they want to use them.

If a sculptor is using marble or wood, the work is usually made by carving and chiselling away the material. Clay and wax are both soft materials which, like a sketch, are sometimes modelled by the artist as a mock up before the sculpture is cast in a harder material such as bronze. Casting is when a hot molten metal is poured in a mould shaped as the artist wants the finished work to appear. An artist may also make an *assemblage* by adding various materials or objects together. An *installation* is a word to describe objects, not necessarily sculptures, placed in a gallery space and sometimes accompanied by sound, special lighting or projected images.

Sofa
by Rita Duffy

Sofa by Rita Duffy

One of the more unusual artworks to be found in the gallery is an extraordinary spiky sofa by the Irish artist Rita Duffy. In this work Rita Duffy has combined everyday objects in an unusual way by threading hundreds of hair clips through the surface of a sofa. The sofa here is an abandoned one she found when she moved into her house in Belfast. When you look from a distance, the sofa appears to have a soft furry texture. However, as you walk nearer, the appearance of the sofa is transformed so that now it looks prickly when viewed up close. You can walk around the sofa and see how the back is also covered in hairclips. Perhaps Rita Duffy's sofa is a nervous sofa and it puts up its prickles to defend itself. In this way you will not want to sit down on it! Rita Duffy is interested in exploring how an object which is familiar and domestic can be transformed into something wild and a bit threatening.

 Can you think of any plants that have prickles to defend themselves or animals whose hair stands on end when they are afraid?

The following are some suggestions:

1. A spiky plant found in the desert. **C** _ _ _ _ _
2. An animal that rolls itself into a ball. **H** _ _ _ _ _ _ _
3. Another type of animal covered in spikes. **P** _ _ _ _ _ _ _ _

Waiting by Kathy Prendergast

This mysterious work shows three women, each without a head and with part of their body missing. Without their complete bodies the women seem quite ghostly. This work has been made with great skill and the women appear to be floating. Their dresses are old fashioned and quite plain. Perhaps the sewing patterns which appear as a backdrop suggest they are seamstresses from the past. The sewing patterns also bring to mind the fact that the women are incomplete. Unlike some sculptures that you can walk around and look at from all sides, *Waiting* is meant to be looked at from the front.

 Kathy Prendergast used fibreglass for the womens' dresses. Fibreglass is a hard and durable material. It is also lightweight and possible to mould into different shapes.

Waiting
by Kathy Prendergast

? Without facial expressions, it is more difficult to see what these women are feeling or thinking. Instead they are communicating with us with their hands. What do their gestures suggest to you? Think of all the different emotions you go through when you are waiting for something. Depending on what it is, you could be eager, excited, anxious, fearful, impatient or hopeful.

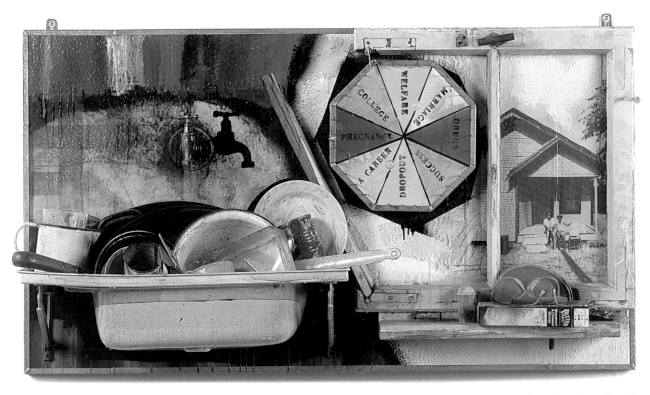

Drawing from 'Tank' by Edward and Nancy Kienholz

This work is a portrait of a different kind. It shows a 'snap-shot' of the life of an American girl called Tank. Tank lived in poverty in Texas. Using a 'wheel of fortune', the artists wanted to show how wealth and, perhaps more importantly, opportunity is unevenly distributed. They also wanted to show how wasteful society can be especially when so many have so little. To make this artwork, Edward and Nancy Kienholz gathered throw away and familiar items from everyday life such as tin cans, pasta packets and dirty dishes stacked in a kitchen sink. A drawing is usually a preparatory work on paper. However, this 'drawing' is a 3D work made as a 'memento' after a larger version of this piece was exhibited.

?

Who can you see through the kitchen window? Maybe that is Tank with her friend, or perhaps they are her neighbours?

Art Activity

MAKE A POP-UP SPIRAL

This great pop-up spiral shape can be used in many ways – for example in a greeting card, a pop-up book or as a 3D picture. The basic shape can be personalised by adding extra pieces of card to create a bumblebee; a ship on the ocean; a solar system; or an abstract composition. The background can be painted like a theatre set to set the scene for your pop-up. The possibilities are endless!

What you need:

* ✳ Good strong cartridge paper or thin card
* ✳ Scissors
* ✳ Sellotape and glue

For decoration:

* ✳ Crayons, paint, coloured paper, coloured pencils (whichever you prefer to use)

Instructions:

* Fold the card in half. (fig.1)

* Take another sheet of card and draw a circle that would fit onto one half of your folded card. (fig.2)

* Cut out the circle.

* Draw a spiral on your circle. It doesn't need to be perfect as all the thick and thin bits can add to the effect.

* Cut out the spiral. (fig.3)

* Place your spiral onto one side of your open card.

* Tape down the outer edge of the spiral.

* Make a loop with a piece of tape, sticky side on the outside and stick to the middle of your spiral. (fig.4)

* Close the card and press firmly down so the tape sticks.

* Open the card - the tape should have attached itself to the opposite page, in the correct position for opening and closing the card smoothly. (fig.5)

* The spiral should expand out. Change the position if you are unhappy with it, then replace the tape with glue or make a small slit in the card and slot the end of the spiral through and stick it to the other side.

* The decoration is up to you. Stick things onto the spiral, paint the page, make lots of spirals on the one page, make a story, make a big book, and use your imagination! (fig.6)

CONTINUED

POP-UP DESIGN

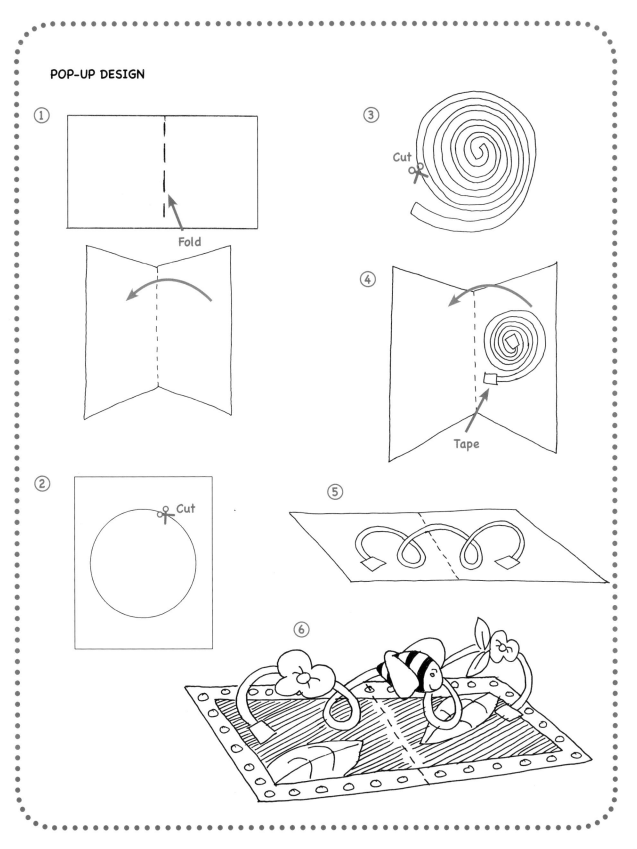

① Fold

② Cut

③ Cut

④ Tape

⑤

⑥

People and Portraits

A portrait is a painting, drawing or sculpture which captures the likeness of a person. Portraits can be full-length, three-quarter length or small head studies.

What can we learn about a person from their portrait? What do their clothes, their expressions and perhaps what they are doing in the painting tell us? Their style of dress may reveal if the work was painted recently or a long time ago. Their clothes can also give us an insight into the fashions current at the time, as well as giving us clues about their social standing. Occasionally, additional items are included in a portrait to tell us more about the sitter. Books, a pen and paper, a globe, or painting equipment, for example, suggest that the sitter may be a writer, a learned person or an artist.

Young Woman with a White Headdress by Edgar Degas

Degas was interested to discover what effect light and shade had on the appearance of the person he was painting. In this lovely painting, a young girl is standing with her back against a brightly-lit window. The light flooding in bathes the girl's face and the room in light and shadow. Her arms are folded and she is holding what seems to be a book or letter in her hand. She seems lost in thought and is perhaps thinking about what she has just read. Little is known as to who she is, but from her dress, she appears to be a countrywoman.

Young Woman with a White Headdress
by Edgar Degas

A Young Breton Girl
by Roderic O'Conor

The Irish artist Roderic O'Conor painted the people and landscape of Brittany on the west coast of France. This painting shows a young girl wearing traditional Breton dress. Because she is in mourning the white collar of her dress is hidden by a black shawl and the ribbons of her headdress are undone. The expression in her eyes and face is sad and quiet and her cheeks are flushed as though she has been crying. The artist uses the gesture of her tightly wrung hands to show the emotion she is feeling inside. The simplicity of this painting makes it more powerful. There are no distracting objects in the background. The young girl is lit by a strong light that casts deep shadows. Even though the colours appear simple - mostly black, white and brown - if you look closely you will see that some of the shadows and background are painted with red and green brushstrokes. Red and green together are not a **harmonious** combination and may have been used by O'Conor to highlight the girl's unsettled state.

A Young Breton Girl
by Roderic O'Conor

Harmonious colours
are those that lie beside each other on the colour wheel. Often these are colour schemes found in nature.

Dockers by Maurice MacGonigal

Dockers was painted by the Irish artist Maurice MacGonigal. It shows men by the quayside in Dublin's docks where they have gathered hoping to be hired for a day's work loading and unloading a cargo ship. This painting was made in 1933–4, during a time when many people found it difficult to find jobs and so were often very poor. Three men, called 'button-men' are standing at the front of the picture. They are waiting to hear if their names will be called from a list of people allowed to work that day. The two men on the left were from Co. Clare.

They had come to Dublin hoping to find work. Do you think they may be missing their families and friends? Perhaps they are worried they may not be hired. The man on the right with his back to us, and smoking a pipe, was from Dublin. He seems less worried, or perhaps has given up caring? Behind the three men is the hustle and bustle of dockers whose names have already been called and who are queuing to start work on the ship. With this painting, the artist may have hoped to raise awareness of the plight of these men.

i

Dockers was not painted on the quayside. The Trade Union leader Jim Larkin sent these three men to pose for this painting in the artist's studio.

Dockers
by Maurice MacGonigal

Tea in the Garden by Walter Osborne

Walter Osborne lived in Castlewood Avenue in Rathmines in Dublin and this painting shows the garden of his neighbours, the Crawfords. Among the people painted here is Miss Crawford who is pouring the tea. She was aged eighteen at the time Walter Osborne painted her in 1902. Sitting on the grass, under the shade of a tree, are two children. The girl looking directly at us was the artist's niece, Violet Stockley. It must be a warm summer's day because a straw hat with black ribbon belonging to one of the girls has been discarded and is lying on the ground. In the background, on the garden bench, is an elderly lady. This may have been the artist's mother, Annie Jane Osborne. Walter Osborne has not painted her in great detail. Why do you think this is? Maybe it is because she is sitting in the shade and it is difficult to see her face clearly? Another reason the painting looks sketchy in some parts is that it is unfinished. If you look closely you can see that some of the bare canvas is visible. Walter Osborne died at a young age of pneumonia in 1903 before he could finish the painting.

Tea in the Garden by Walter Osborne with detail below

> ● Walter Osborne painted for many years in France and this painting shows the influence of French Impressionist painters such as Claude Monet and Berthe Morisot.

Art Activity

MAKING LARGE-SCALE PORTRAITS

What you need:
* A2 sheets of coloured sugar paper
* Black charcoal sticks
* White chalk
* Small mirror

Instructions:

* Start by having a good look at the face you intend to draw. If it is a self-portrait you will need a small mirror. Otherwise get a friend or family member to sit facing you. You will notice that the head is wider at the top and tapers towards the chin. The eyes appear about half-way down. The bottom of the nose divides the lower half of the face in two and the mouth is about halfway between the bottom of the nose and the chin. Look at the ears: the tops are in line with the eyes.

* Carefully observe the hairline and how the hair falls around the face. Then look at the neck and shoulders: the neck is nearly as wide as the head.

* Begin your drawing by very lightly drawing in the basic head shape. Try to make it fill the page. Then you can lightly put in lines where you think the eyes, nose and mouth might be. Curve the lines slightly because the face is rounded.

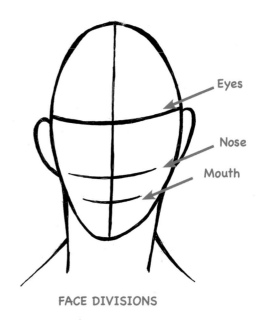

FACE DIVISIONS

Eyes

Nose

Mouth

* Looking at your model or reflection all the time, draw in the features using stronger, bolder strokes. Observe the shadows on the face and fill them in with more strokes or a little smudging. You could fill in the background to make the face stand out. When you have nearly finished the drawing, look again for the lightest parts of the face and hair and use the white chalk to highlight these areas, bringing your portrait to life.

This portrait was made during a Sunday Sketching workshop.

Townscapes and Landscapes

Both urban and rural life, though very different from each other, are full of fascinating subjects and views to capture the imagination of artists.

Waterloo Bridge by Claude Monet

Claude Monet liked to paint the same subject, or motif, again and again but at different times of the day and at different times of the year. This was to see how weather and atmospheric conditions such as snow or fog, pale morning light or the blaze of a setting sun could dramatically change the appearance of something. *Waterloo Bridge* was painted while Monet was in London. Monet liked the fog and grime of London because it blurred the outline of objects and structures making them appear less solid. Monet also loved painting water. In France he had a studio boat from which he painted scenes which caught his attention. The pale

Waterloo Bridge
by Claude Monet

pink wisps and cold blue of *Waterloo Bridge* suggest that it may be an early morning view of the famous bridge. In the background, smoke pours out from tall chimney stacks while Waterloo Bridge itself is crowded with horse drawn carriages. Although this painting appears quite blurry when viewed close up, the bridge appears 'in-focus' and more solid when looked at from a distance.

Boulevard Raspail by Roderic O'Conor

Roderic O'Conor was descended from one of the ancient Irish families of Co. Roscommon. Like many of his fellow artists, he left Ireland to continue his art education in Antwerp and Paris. O'Conor lived for a time in Brittany where he painted the people and countryside there. In 1904 the artist returned to Paris. This painting, *Boulevard Raspail*, shows the main street in Montparnasse, a district in the south of Paris. In the background are two tall structures that look like cranes. Perhaps some construction activity is underway. Roderic O'Conor's studio was very close to Boulevard Raspail so this painting shows a street he knew well. In this painting you can see O'Conor's very distinctive striped style of painting. These stripes may have been influenced by the paintings of Van Gogh whose work the artist was aware of. Roderic O'Conor also knew Paul Gauguin, a painter known for his use of vibrant and dramatic contrasts of colour. This night-time scene has a mysterious atmosphere. None of the faces of the couples walking down the hill is visible. Their long cloaks and hunched poses suggest a cold winter's evening. Rounding the bend, however, a bright streetlamp bathes them in welcome light.

Boulevard Raspail
by Roderic O'Conor

Lakeside Cottages
by Paul Henry

Lakeside Cottages by Paul Henry

This picture of cottages beside a lake was painted in 1929 by the Irish artist Paul Henry. Paul Henry lived in Achill for a number of years and he loved to paint the landscape and people of the West of Ireland. The cottages in this painting were made of mud and stone with bright white walls and a thatched roof. The thatch kept the houses nice and warm and was gathered from dried straw. Look how small the windows in these cottages are. As well as glass being expensive, this was to keep the cottages as cosy as possible as the only source of heat was from the open fire.

The dark mounds outside each of the cottages is turf which each family would cut from the bog. Because these cottages had no electricity, turf was a very important source of fuel which kept the fire in the cottage burning. The fire not only kept

everyone warm and dry, it was also used for cooking. The door to the cottage may have been a half-door. This meant that the bottom half of the door could stay closed to keep the farm animals out while the top part could be opened to let in light. You could also lean out and chat with your neighbours as they passed by. Paul Henry liked using simple shapes in his paintings. In this painting we see the curved shape of the blue mountains, the zig zag path leading to the cottage closest to us, the circular mounds of turf and the triangular shape of the gable wall of the cottages.

Most of all, Paul Henry loved painting big skies. In this painting, the billowing clouds coming in from the Atlantic Ocean and bringing lots of fresh air take up more than half the painting. However, it does seem like a nice sunny day and the lake is so calm it looks like a mirror.

Perspective: When artists want to show distance in their paintings, they use something called perspective. When an object is closer to you it looks bigger and things further away appear smaller even though they are often the same actual size.

Atmospheric perspective can also create a sense of distance by using colours which are richer and deeper closest to us and those that are lighter for objects or landscapes further away.

Look at how Paul Henry paints his cottages. They are all arranged so they appear to be getting smaller. It is possible to draw a straight line connecting their chimneys and this is how Paul Henry drew them in perspective.

Close
by Elizabeth Magill

Close and Grayscale (2) by Elizabeth Magill

Grayscale (2) and *Close* are both by the contemporary Irish artist Elizabeth Magill. Elizabeth Magill really enjoys painting landscapes and they appear frequently as a subject in her work. She was born in Ontario, in Canada but moved to Antrim, in Northern Ireland with her family when she was young. The memory of the landscape around where she lived as a youngster has continued to inspire her imagination. She is also influenced by 19th century Romantic landscape painting, especially by the German artist Caspar David Friedrich. His paintings are quite moody and dramatic and often show isolated places.

Elizabeth Magill's paintings are also very atmospheric and are often quite mysterious, as you can see in both these paintings. Using mostly shades of purple, *Close* shows houses at twilight at the edge of a wood. The houses, electricity pole and wires are immediately recognisable as being from the world around us today. The dark trees are silhouetted against the big, bright sky. Lights have come on in some of the houses and the first stars are beginning to twinkle. She really captures the clear sky and coolness of what seems to be an autumnal evening.

Elizabeth Magill sometimes uses collage in her paintings. She likes to pour diluted, thin paint onto her canvas letting the dripping paint flow wherever it likes. She also adds little pieces of glittering rhinestone to make her stars glimmer and suddenly appear as light shines on them.

Grayscale (2) is a magical landscape. Like *Close*, this painting is almost like a photograph because the misty landscape and delicate branches look so real. Photographs often give Elizabeth Magill the first ideas for her painting. The colours in this painting are mostly shades of grey except for some green and yellow blobs that light up the atmospheric wood and sky like shooting stars, fairy lanterns or flitting fireflies.

Grayscale (2)
by Elizabeth Magill

Contemporary art describes art that is made very recently or at the current time.

Art Activity

A TEXTURED LANDSCAPE

What you need:

* Sand, flour, shells, cotton wool
* Charcoal, coloured chalks, pencils, crayons for making rubbings
* Collected materials like newspapers, magazines, plastics, dried leaves and flowers
* Mixed papers
* Thick paper or card for your painting
* Glue to attach found items

The drawing on the left was inspired by Honolulu Garden by Mary Swanzy. Lots of flour was added to the painting on the right to create a textured landscape.

Instructions:

* Looking at a landscape painting you really like and admire, explore the different textures the painter uses to show how the land changes, and how the light varies throughout the scene. Then organise the materials which you have gathered from light to dark and with variation of colour. This will help you see how they can be used throughout your picture.

* A great way to add texture to your paint is to add some sand. Slowly mix in the sand, seeing how much best creates the effect that you want. It will make your paint lumpy and bumpy. Another way to use the sand would be to mix it with PVA glue and paint it onto the paper in the areas which you want to be particularly textured. If there are rocks in the foreground, sand would be a good option to give a rough texture.

* If perhaps there was a river, some flour may be the best choice as it thickens up your paint, so that you can give a real sense of the river flowing.

* Another good way of adding some texture to your picture is to take some **rubbings**. Go outside and find some interesting surfaces, like the bark of a tree or the grooves in a path. To make a good rubbing, take a sheet of paper and place it over the object. Using a crayon, pencil, charcoal or coloured chalk, lightly rub over the paper's surface repeatedly until the texture of what is below becomes clear on your page.

CONTINUED ▶▶

- You could also add texture to your landscape by adding some things that you have found, like shells, leaves or flowers. Some cotton wool, pulled apart, could make great clouds or foliage for trees if you painted it green. You could also add bits and pieces of photographs you have found in magazines. Create a collage out of lots of different textures: some shiny and polished when you touch them and some gritty and sandy.

Leaf Rubbings

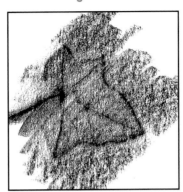

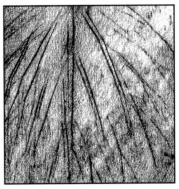

SAMPLE RUBBINGS

Bark Rubbing

Focus on Abstract Paintings

Not all painting or sculpture tells a story or is of something that we can immediately recognise from the world around us. Some paintings are just made up of one colour or show only shapes and patterns. These are called abstract paintings.

Artists sometimes try to capture the mood and atmosphere of something by using only colour, shapes and patterns rather than by describing a person, object or landscape in detail. The surface and paint texture can play important roles in abstract paintings. Sometimes an abstract artist wants you to see how the work was painted by using obvious brushstrokes and by applying the paint in a very expressive way. At other times, abstract artists attempt to apply paint as smoothly as possible so that the surface of the painting is completely flat.

Black Relief over Yellow and Orange
by Ellsworth Kelly

Black Relief over Yellow and Orange by Ellsworth Kelly

The American artist Ellsworth Kelly is inspired by fragments from the world around him. Examples of these fragments include the shape of a shadow or the space between objects. Like a jigsaw, his abstract paintings are occasionally made up of simple shapes which can be re-arranged to create a completely different abstract painting. In this painting *Black Relief over Yellow and Orange* there are three panels, each of which is painted in a different colour. Ellsworth Kelly prefers his paintings to be completely flat so that you cannot see any brushstrokes.

i

Relief describes something which projects forward from the surface

Untitled No. 7
by Agnes Martin

Untitled No. 7 by Agnes Martin

The Canadian artist Agnes Martin uses very pale colours in this square painting. When this painting was first bought by the gallery in 1980 some people asked why the gallery had bought a blank canvas! At first this painting seems completely bare. However, if you look closely at it for a while you will see bands of horizontal lines of very pale blue and cream. Agnes Martin was thinking of large areas of open countryside when she was painting this picture. In North America and Canada there are huge areas called prairies where all you can see for miles around are wire fences one after another far into the distance. Like some other abstract artists, Agnes Martin takes something familiar and recognisable from everyday life and simplifies it by using colour, shapes and patterns. In this way Agnes Martin captures what is for her the most striking aspect of the landscape she is looking at.

Wall of Light Orange Yellow by Sean Scully

Sean Scully was born in Dublin but grew up in London where he went to art college. He moved to America, and following studies at Harvard University, he set up a studio in New York. Sean Scully uses horizontal and vertical stripes in his abstract paintings. He believes that the combination of stripes, colours and the way paint is applied can express many different moods. His abstract paintings are inspired by people he knows or everyday objects such as walls, doors or windows. In this way familiar things, such as the way light may fall, cracks, shadows or rough edges, are magnified. Scully's paintings are usually quite large in scale. Together with their size and their animated brushstrokes, the colour combinations he uses give these paintings a powerful emotional impact.

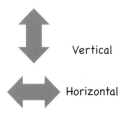

Vertical

Horizontal

Wall of Light Orange Yellow
by Sean Scully

Recoil by Mark Francis

Mark Francis is fascinated by how objects such as plants look under a microscope. A microscope allows you to see the network of veins which bring nutrients to all parts of the plant. You could also imagine that the frantic curves in his painting are a birds eye view of a town or overlapping roads at a spaghetti-junction. Even though there is very little colour, this is an action packed painting full of energy, movement and rhythm.

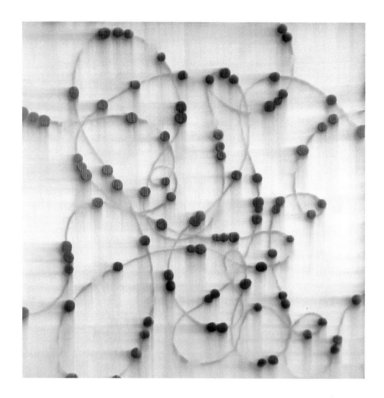

Recoil
by Mark Francis

Art Activity

MAKE AN ABSTRACT PAINTING INSPIRED BY THE WORLD AROUND YOU.

- Ideas for your abstract painting could come from the view outside your window. Look at the shapes of the buildings, trees, electricity wires, poles and other things that you see around you. To make a view finder to focus in on a particular view, take a piece of A4 paper card and cut a rectangular shape so that a border of around 5 cm is left. Use this rectangular shape to 'frame' your view.

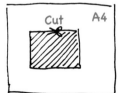

- Looking around you maybe you can see the same shape repeated over and over e.g. rectangular panes of windows, front doors in a terrace of houses, a brick wall, the pattern of tree branches, or the criss-cross of a wire fence.

- Without using any detail, draw the outline shape of the things you see. Use these shapes and repeating patterns as the basis for your abstract drawing or painting. Combine these simple shapes in different ways to create several abstract works. Decide what colours you would like to use. Will you use many colours, or choose a limited palette?

Film and Photography

The development of technology has created exciting possibilities for artists who want to experiment with new ways of making art and of expressing their ideas. Film, video, sound, neon and digital photography are just some of the new media used by artists in recent years. When an artist uses film or photography it can sometimes make the subject appear more real. However, occasionally photographs or films may be just as staged or composed as a painting.

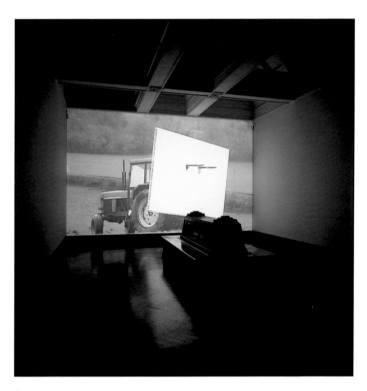

Screen
by Matt Calderwood

FILM PROJECTIONS

Film, video, DVD and digital photography are among the most innovative inventions of the 20th century and artists have explored the potential of film in earnest over the last 30 years. One of the advantages of film is the important role sound can play. The artist can also choose to work in black and white or colour, while a fleeting event or conversation can be captured using film and replayed over and over again.

Screen by Matt Calderwood

This piece, which is called *Screen*, was made especially for projection onto a wall in this gallery. The artist wanted to create an element of surprise in this work and he certainly succeeds! The video starts with a brightly lit blank white wall. We all wonder what is going to happen. In the background there are sounds of birds singing. What are these birds doing in the gallery? All of a sudden two metal arms seem to tear through the gallery wall. The wall is then lifted up to reveal a country field behind. As the wall continues to rise upwards we see that the wall is being carried away on a forklift. Where there was once a gallery wall we have now been transported to the artist's family farm in County Antrim. In this way, the artist uses video to play a visual joke, leading us to question our ideas of the solidity of objects such as walls and the reality of the space around us.

PHOTOGRAPHY

At the Border II (Low Visibility) by Willie Doherty

Willie Doherty was born in Derry and much of his work explores the political conflict in the North of Ireland. This photograph shows the headlights of a car shining on what appears to be an empty country road. The title of the work suggests that it is near the border between the Republic of Ireland and Northern Ireland. In this work, boundaries and surveillance are hinted at, but not actually seen. This is a large-scale photographic print. When shown in the gallery, this work is deliberately hung close to the floor. In this way the low viewpoint makes

At the Border II
(Low Visibility)
by Willie Doherty

it seem that you are in the car looking out on this dark road with the headlights coming towards you. The image is printed on very glossy photographic paper on aluminium. This makes the photograph seem like a mirror that reflects anyone looking at it. Willie Doherty said that the advantage of using photography was that he had to get out of his studio to find his subject taken from real life.

Invisible Cities: Mist, Interior II, Untitled (Woman) by Paul Seawright

From left to right:
Invisible Cities:
Mist
Interior II
Untitled (Woman)
by Paul Seawright

In his photographic series on the theme of *Invisible Cities*, Paul Seawright explores the urban sprawl of large cities on the African continent and the huge numbers of people living on the margins in dire poverty. Despite their size, many of these cities remain a mystery to most of us. These photographs are thought-provoking because they are suggestive rather than trying to tell a story. By obscuring details, as in *Mist,* or showing half-hidden interiors, the photographs create an uneasy atmosphere and a sense of uncertainty. Are these places as dangerous as they seem or is it just because they are unfamiliar that we are afraid?

The Ballymun photography project is an after school photography club with children from Holy Spirit Boys and Holy Spirit Girls National Schools. Under the direction of photographer and film-maker Perry Ogden, the children learn about photography using 35mm cameras while documenting the dramatic changes to their urban environment. This striking photograph was taken by Karl Dawson.

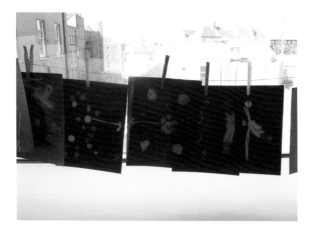 

These photograms were made using found items and a photographic enlarger during summer art camps for children at the gallery.

Art Activity

HOW TO MAKE A PINHOLE CAMERA

Making a pinhole camera is a very good way of introducing yourself to the basic workings of a camera and the importance of light in creating your image.

This art activity definitely requires adult help and supervision.

What you need:
* Tin box (eg. sweet tin/biscuit tin)
* Sandpaper
* Ruler and pencil
* Black card
* Black paint
* Paint brush
* Small needle
* Black tape
* Blu-tack
* Heavy object such as a hammer
* A darkened room with as little white light as possible – blinds or black bags could help to block out light.
* A clock with a seconds hand.
* String and pegs to hang photographs from while they dry.

The following equipment should be available from all good photographic shops:
* Photographic paper
* Photographic developer and fixer
* 3 trays for photographic chemicals
* Tongs
* A photographic safety light

Instructions:

Making the pinhole camera

* First of all sand the inside and lid of the tin, then paint it black and allow to dry. Use the ruler and pencil to find and mark the centre point on one side of the tin. Using a heavy object such as a hammer, make a small pinprick using the needle. Make a shutter 3cm square with the black card and tape over the pin prick using the black tape. In a dark room with the safety light on, secure the photographic paper in the tin on the side opposite to the pinhole (emulsion side facing the pinhole) with the blu-tack.

Taking a photograph

* On a bright day, place the camera in front of the subject and remove the shutter. Do not hold the camera as you will get camera shake. You will have to experiment with the timing but usually about 3 or 4 minutes on a bright day should be okay. Remember to tape back the shutter when finished taking the photograph.

Processing the photograph

* Mix the developer and fixer according to the manufacturer's instructions and place in separate trays. Label the three trays: developer, stop-bath (ordinary water) and fixer.

CONTINUED

- In a dark room using only the safety light, open the camera, take out the photographic paper and place in the developer and watch your photograph appear! Leave it in developer for 2 minutes and gently rock the tray.

- Using tongs, take out the photograph and place it in the stop-bath for 20 seconds. Finally put the photograph in the fixer and leave for 5 minutes. Wash the photograph in water and hang to dry on your photograph 'washing line.'

Problems?
- If your photograph is completely black it could mean that light is leaking into your camera.

- If your photograph is too light you need to increase the length of exposure.

> **i** Photo comes from the Greek word for light.

PINHOLE CAMERA

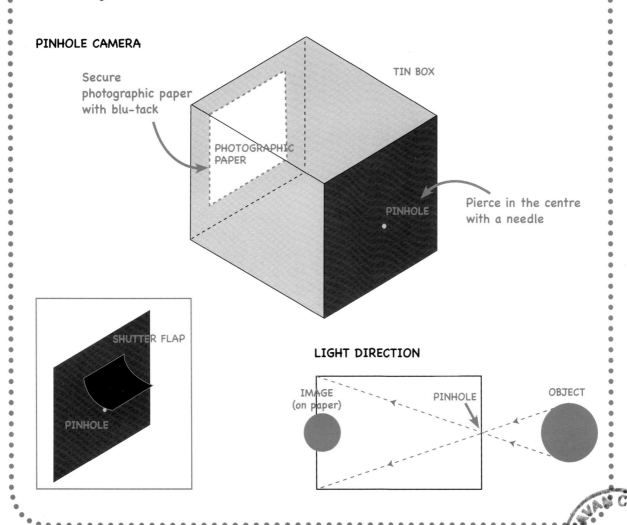

Secure photographic paper with blu-tack

TIN BOX

PHOTOGRAPHIC PAPER

PINHOLE

Pierce in the centre with a needle

SHUTTER FLAP

PINHOLE

LIGHT DIRECTION

IMAGE (on paper) — PINHOLE — OBJECT

Index of Artists

Page numbers are included to help you find the artworks in the book.

RODERIC O'CONOR
b. Milltown, Co. Roscommon, 1860 –
d. Neuil-sur-Layon, France, 1940
Boulevard Raspail
Oil on canvas, 52 x 60 cm
© Estate of Roderic O'Conor
page 81

PERRY OGDEN
b. Shropshire, 1961
Interior Francis Bacon Studio, 7 Reece Mews, 1998
Photograph on aluminium, 122 x 152.5 cm
© Perry Ogden
page 18

WILLIAM ORPEN
b. Dublin, 1878 – d. London, 1931
Hugh Lane Reading
Pencil on paper, 22.9 x 17.7 cm
page 25

WILLIAM ORPEN
b. Dublin, 1878 – d. London, 1931
Reflections: China and Japan, 1902
Oil on canvas, 40.5 x 51 cm
Lane Gift, 1912
page 35

WALTER OSBORNE
b. Dublin, 1859 – d. Dublin, 1903
Boy on Shore, 1886
Oil on board, 15.3 x 22.8 cm
Bequest of the late Canon Charles Edward Osborne, 1971
page 57

WALTER OSBORNE
b. Dublin, 1859 – d. Dublin, 1903
Tea in the Garden, 1902
Oil on canvas, 132 x 217 cm
Lane Gift, 1912
page 77

KATHY PRENDERGAST
b. Dublin, 1958
Waiting, 1980
Fibre glass, resin, parquet flooring and sewing patterns, 184 x 230 cm
Courtesy of the artist and The Kerlin Gallery, Dublin
© Kathy Prendergast
page 70

AUGUSTE RENOIR
b. Limoges, 1841– Cagnes, 1919
The Umbrellas (Les Parapluies), c. 1881-86
Oil on canvas, 180.3 x 114.9 cm
Sir Hugh Lane Bequest, 1917
© Trustees National Gallery, London
page 16

BRITON RIVIERE
b. London, 1840 – d. London, 1920
Studies of an Irish Wolfhound
Pastel on paper, 56 x 70 cm
Presented by the artist
page 26

GEORGE RUSSELL (AE)
b. Lurgan, Co. Armagh, 1867 – d. Bournemouth, 1935
The Winged Horse, 1904
Oil on board, 31.5. x 45.8 cm
Lane Gift, 1912
page 51

NIKI DE SAINT PHALLE
b. Neuilly-sur-Seine, France, 1930 – San Diego, USA, 2002
Big Bird, 1982
Polyester polychrome, 160 x 150 x 99 cm
© ADAGP, Paris and DACS, London 2006
page 43

JOHN SINGER SARGENT
b. Florence, 1856 – d. London, 1925
Portrait of Hugh Lane, 1906
Oil on canvas, 74.3 x 62.2 cm
Lane Bequest, 1913
page 10

JOHN SINGER SARGENT
b. Florence, 1856 – d. London, 1925
Portrait of Miss Anstruther Thomson
Charcoal on paper, 34.4 x 23.5 cm
Presented by Annabel Blackburne, 1942
page 19

PATRICK SCOTT
b. Kilbritten, Co. Cork, 1921
Large Solar Device, 1964
Tempera on unprimed canvas, 234 x 153 cm
Presented by the Contemporary Irish Art Society, 1964
© Patrick Scott
page 67

SEAN SCULLY
b. Dublin, 1945
Wall of Light Orange Yellow, 2000
Oil on linen, 274.3 x 335.3 cm
Presented by the artist, 2006
Courtesy of the artist and The Kerlin Gallery, Dublin
© Sean Scully
page 90

PAUL SEAWRIGHT
b. Belfast, 1965
Invisible Cities: Mist, Interior II, Untitled (Woman), 2005
Lightjet print on fuji crystal paper, mounted on aluminium, 127 x 152.4 cm
Courtesy of the artist and The Kerlin Gallery, Dublin
© Paul Seawright
page 94

EDOUARD VUILLARD
b. Cuiseaux, 1868 – d. La Baule, France, 1940
The Mantlepiece (La Chiminée), 1905
Oil on cardboard, 51.4 x 77.5 cm
Sir Hugh Lane Bequest, 1917
© Trustees National Gallery, London
page 16
© ADAGP, Paris and DACS, London 2007.

JAMES MCNEILL WHISTLER
b. Lowell, Massachusetts, 1834 – d. London, 1903
The Artist's Studio, 1865
Oil on cardboard, 62.2 x 46.3 cm
Lane Gift, 1912
page 20

JACK B. YEATS
b. London, 1871 – d. Dublin, 1957
The Accordion Player
Watercolour on paper, 53.5 x 37 cm
Presented by the artist
© Estate of Jack B. Yeats / DACS, London 2006
page 40

JACK B. YEATS
b. London, 1871 – d. Dublin, 1957
The Travelling Circus
Watercolour on paper, 27 x 36 cm
Bequeathed by Josephine Webb, 1924.
© Estate of Jack B. Yeats / DACS, London 2006
page 46

JACK B. YEATS
b. London, 1871 – d. Dublin, 1957
There is No Night, 1949
Oil on canvas, 102 x 153 cm
© Estate of Jack B. Yeats / DACS, London 2006
page 35

Artworks purchased by Dublin City Gallery The Hugh Lane unless otherwise stated.
The publisher and author have made every effort to trace the copyright holders of the illustrations reproduced in this book; they will be happy to correct in subsequent editions any errors or omissions that are brought to their attention.

Glossary

Abstract Art describes art which is made up of colours, shapes or patterns rather than showing a recognisable likeness.

Assemblage describes the piecing together of a collection of objects to form an artwork.

Collage describes the process of gluing cut pieces of paper, photographs and other everyday objects together on to paper or canvas creating a mix and match artwork.

Composition is a word to describe how a picture is arranged, where the objects or people are placed and what is chosen to be included.

Conceptual Art is art where the idea of something is paramount and usually conveyed in a very minimalist way.

Contemporary Art describes art made very recently or at the current time.

Figurative Art describes art with a recognisable subject, usually depicting people.

Installation describes an artwork, usually three-dimensional, located in the gallery space. It can be made up of several objects, of different sizes and medium.

Landscape describes images of the countryside.

Medium is the word to describe the materials used by the artist. For example, oil paint, watercolour, chalk and so on. A mixed media artwork uses a combination of different materials.

Minimalism Art using very simple materials with the barest detail.

Modern Art describes art from the mid-19th century onwards which broke with tradition by trying to show things in a new way.

Mosaic describes patterns made by joining together little pieces of stone or glass of different colours.

Multi-media describes artworks that include sound, film or other forms of technology.

Oil paint is made by grinding pigment in oil. It is quite a thick type of paint which dries very slowly.

Painting This is a representation on a flat surface such as canvas, paper or wood.

Palette is an object which the artist uses to hold and mix their colours. A palette knife has a thin steel blade for mixing paint or applying paint to the surface.

Perspective is a way of showing distance and depth in a drawing or painting.

Pigment is colour from natural or artificial sources which can be mixed with binding material such as oil, enabling the artist to use it.

Portrait describes a picture of a person.

Profile describes a view of a person turned to the side so only half their face is visible.

Primary colours Red, yellow and blue are the three primary colours.

Scale describes the size of something e.g. large scale or small scale, particularly in relation to other objects or its surroundings.

Sculpture is a three-dimensional artwork usually made of stone, marble, wood, steel or glass.

Secondary colours The three secondary colours are purple, orange and green. They are made by mixing primary colours together.

Still-life describes paintings of everyday objects such as flowers, fruit or jugs.

Style describes the way an artist paints.

Subject This is what is shown and what the work is about.

Viewer This is the person looking at the artwork.

Watercolour This is pigment mixed with water rather than oil.

Select Bibliography

Baldwin, B., *Looking into the Tate,* London 1997

Bourke, M., *Exploring Art at the National Gallery,* Dublin 1997

Cappock, M.(ed.) et al, *Dublin City Gallery The Hugh Lane: Guide to the Collection,* Dublin 2006

Charman, H. and Wilson, G., *Tate Modern: Teacher's Kit,* London 2001

Hickey, N., *The Art of Looking,* Cork 2006

Malaguzzi, L., *The Hundred Languages of Children,* Reggio Emilia 1997

O'Connell, D., *Picture This: Looking at Art in the Hugh Lane Municipal Gallery of Modern Art*, Dublin 1997

O'Donnell, J., *Kidsguide to the Francis Bacon Studio*, Dublin 2001

O'Donoghue, H., and Davoren, A., *A Space to Grow: New approaches to working with children, primary school teachers and contemporary art in the context of a museum,* Dublin 1999

Paul, S., Twentieth Century Art: A Resource for Educators, New York 1999

Penny, N., *National Gallery London Pocket Guides: Frames,* London 2005

Richardson, J., *Looking at Pictures: An Introduction to art for young people through the collection of the National Gallery London,* London 1997

Sousa, J., *Looking at Art Together: Process Catalogue and Parent Guide,* Chicago 2002

Sousa, J., *Faces, Places and Inner Spaces: A Guide to Looking at Art,* Chicago 2006